A Canopy of Light and Love

Alan Kolp

Friends United Press
Richmond, Indiana
47374

A Canopy of Light and Love

Library of Congress Cataloging-in-Publication Data

Kolp, Alan, 1944-
    A Canopy of Light and Love/by Alan Kolp.
      p. cm.
    ISBN 0-944350-26-7
    1. Christian life--Quaker authors. I. Title
BV4501.2.K62 1993
248.4'896--dc20   93-16037
                                                                             CIP

Graphic Art
    Jeffrey Dowers
    Susanna Combs

A Canopy of Light and Love

by Alan Kolp

*Dedication
to Christina Ann Kolp
My Daughter*

TABLE OF CONTENTS

Preface

Introduction

Chapter 1 — Seasons

Chapter 2 — Revelation

Chapter 3 — Wisdom

Chapter 4 — Pilgrimage

Chapter 5 — Emotions and Moods

Chapter 6 — The Heart of Love

Chapter 7 — Places of Nurture

Chapter 8 — Grace

Chapter 9 — Free From / Free For

Chapter 10 — Suffering

Conclusion

PREFACE

This book has evolved since 1984 as a series of essays which appeared in *Quaker Life*. The opportunity to write monthly has brought to me the challenge to pay attention to myself and others in order to see how God is present in and through lives. Paying attention is key to any spiritual experience. Spirituality is the lived experience of this present and presenting God. These essays are bits of reflection on spirituality as I have observed the lived experience in many people.

Authors of books typically thank others for assistance. Gratitude must be offered especially in the case of this book. Without other people—both historically and contemporarily—this book simply would not have come into being. Particularly, I thank the many unnamed friends for sharing their lives with me—for allowing me to pay attention to their lived experience and discern God's present hand.

Specifically, I thank three editors of Quaker Life over a period of eight years, 1984-1992. To Jack Kirk who initially asked me to write, Stanley Banker, Jr. who humorously encouraged me on and James Newby who has continued as friend and fellow-traveler, I express my gratitude. Carol Beals, Managing Editor of *Quaker Life*, gently has made me aware "another one" (article) is due and patiently waited for my response. I also owe a word of appreciation to Ardith Talbot, Editor and Manager of Friends United Press. Ardith has been receptive, co-operative and helpful. Finally, a very special word of gratitude to two people who have been crucial to the process of moving ideas into print. Sue Kern, my colleague at Earlham School of Religion, and Wayne Copenhaver, my associate at First Friends Meeting, have shared generously of their time, energy and talent to bring this book to fruition.

With words of appreciation expressed, I now have the deepest delight to dedicate the book. This book is dedicated to my younger daughter, Christina Ann Kolp. Her determination to ride a bicycle inspired one of these essays. The spirit of that determination permeates these pages. Although Christina is my daughter, she also has been my teacher! She has allowed me to mature enough to realize being a professor of spirituality means finally being taught by children of the Spirit.

Christina—my coquettish daughter—smart, stylish and spirited: to you this book is dedicated. You have lived under my roof, but we both live under the canopy of light and love!

The Feast of Epiphany
1993

INTRODUCTION

"Most people live their entire lives in monotone. There is sound, but no rhythm or beat; there is color, but no vibrancy or pattern. God, self, and others remain hidden. We look, but we do not see; we hear, but do not listen; we feel, but do not experience; we think, but do not understand. The burning bushes are never even approached."

These words from physician-spiritual guide, Kenneth Bakken, are found in a chapter entitled, "Living In Neutral." They offer a sad commentary on contemporary life. <u>Living in neutral is the condemnation of routine</u> — rather than the freedom routine can bring. We are condemned when we arise in the morning, only ready to "go through the motions." There is sound, but no rhythm or beat.

There is no movement when in neutral. The vibrancy of life is blocked. The bounce has gone flat. Shoulders are drooped, eyes are sad and backs bent. In this state we are existing under a canopy of darkness and apathy. But, the good news is the gift of possibility — possibility actualized as light and love. To embrace this possibility is to come to live under a canopy of light and love.

This image of canopy comes from an eighteenth century Quaker, Job Scott, as he described a gathered group of worshippers who experienced the descent of the divine Spirit covering them. This image can be extended to describe our lives daily lived under this canopy. This covering of the divine Spirit is better than a hat—but we do have to remember to put it on!

To live under this canopy of light and love is to "put life in gear." Monotony gives way to variety and boredom is recharged with interest because we become engaged. Routine becomes freeing. Condemnation becomes validation. We feel the beat in life. We understand and appreciate the gift of learning— even learning to ride bicycles! Riding a bicycle seems so easy for us who have done it for years. The frustration — and sometimes agony — in the learning process is a faded memory. In the process of teaching my daughter how to ride—and failing as a teacher—I learned another lesson: my teaching depended on her readiness. One day she was ready . . . and another kid taught her! Another lesson given to me the teacher: <u>learning and teaching is a community enterprise.</u>

Probably, most of the learning about humanity and God does not come in classrooms. Normally, classrooms are too formal and artificial. Rather, the whole world is God's classroom and we all are the students. We are students because we are disciples. To be a disciple is to become a student of Jesus.

Jesus was first a rabbi, a teacher, going about in this worldly classroom. His gift was the *extra-ordinary* offered in the midst of the ordinary. Instead of mediocrity, his gift was immortality; instead of death, life. Our call to follow Jesus really is nothing more than a call to receive this gift. The gift is the gospel—the possibility of living under the canopy of light and love.

To live under this canopy of light and love is not a means of protecting ourselves from the world. In fact, the opposite is the case. The gift of the gospel is a call to *imitatio Christi* —to imitate Christ. As Jesus was in the world, so will we be in the world. Authentic spirituality is lived in the world, but with a transforming sense that we are not "of the world." In his book, *The Transforming Moment,* James Loder gives a clue to where this transforming sense leads. "The experiences we want eventually to understand in *Christian* terms are precisely those that reopen the question of reality because the subject of the experience has been convicted by a Spiritual Presence far greater than the subject him - or herself." The canopy of light and love, then, offers not protection so much as presence and perseverance. The transforming sense which students of Jesus take into the world is the capacity and willingness to "reopen the question of reality."

This reopening is precisely what Jesus was about. As Marcus Borg puts it in *Jesus: A New Vision*, "he sought the transformation of his social world." Borg develops the image of Jesus which offers clear direction for the twenty-first century students of Jesus. "First, there is a dimension of reality beyond the visible world of our ordinary experience, a dimension charged with power, whose ultimate quality is compassion. Second, the fruits of a life lived in accord with the Spirit are to be embodied not only in individuals, but also in the life of the faithful community." As Jesus' disciples, we are always reopening the question of reality when we look for and live with the awareness of that other dimension of reality beyond the visible and the ordinary.

The essays in this book are just such reopenings. They are experiential—lived life—but experiential with a sense for the dimension of the Spirit as it is reflected through the visible and the ordinary. They were written over a period of time—but experience always happens at some time and in some place. Whether one is aware of perfectionism or perfume, there is always the possibility of seeing and knowing that dimension of reality beyond the ordinary. The Spirit beckons us to look, to see, and, then, to perceive.

These essays are the same invitation. They beckon you to look around and pay attention. Paying attention is the move from looking to seeing. You have a focus in seeing. The ordinary level of reality is now ready to be reopened. Seeing leads to perceiving. At the level of perception the spiritual dimension of reality is revealed. As students of the Spirit, we learn more about life's depth and breadth. We are lovingly and gracefully taught about God and about ourselves and about each other. In the process we are transformed from children of the world to children of God.

As children of God, we are brought under the canopy of light and love. There we are nourished and nurtured. We grow in spiritual stature and wisdom. We are called to carry this light into the darkness of our world. We are exhorted to incarnate this love in a world of enmity. We can do this because under the canopy of light and love we are given a vision—a vision of "a new heaven and a new earth." (Rev. 21:1) This vision can be lived out here and now under the canopy of light and love.

In the summer of 1789 the Rhode Island Quietist Quaker, Job Scott, wrote his wife from Holly Spring, North Carolina. Scott was on a preaching mission and powerfully shares his experiences. There is an overall depressive tone to much of his writing, but in this letter he uses compelling language. He describes the work of the "pure power of the word of life." Indeed, Scott understood himself and his work to be an instrument of this pure power.

The speaking forth of this word had its effect which Scott elaborates with lovely descriptive language. He says "in many meetings, especially where the most are not Friends, the canopy of light and love, in brightness and in awful-weight, spreads over us, through nearly or quite the whole meeting." The imagery of a "canopy" is the leading image not only for this quotation and this chapter, but for this whole book. This book uses essays to describe everyday people and events to portray how God continues to spread a canopy of light and love over all.

The spiritual essence of the image of the canopy is significant. The canopy consists of light and love. The biblical tradition explicitly affirms God to be both light and love. Therefore, the canopy which spreads over us is God's presence! The spreading of the canopy opens us to the divine light and brings us into the divine love. With the Psalmist we declare God to be "my light and my salvation; whom shall I fear?" (Ps. 27:1) The prophet Isaiah describes the spiritual confidence which comes upon those of us brought out of darkness into the canopy of light. Isaiah proclaims, "the people who walked in darkness have seen a great light; and those who dwelt in a land of deep darkness, on them has light shined." (Isa. 9:2)

George Fox, founder of Quakerism, had a vision of a great people to be gathered; Job Scott declares this great people will be gathered under the canopy of light and love. Under this canopy we will see and be seen—love and be loved. The fourteenth century Greek Orthodox theologian, Gregory of Palamas, gives depth to this canopy experience. Expectantly, he suggests that God's chosen disciples will see "the essential and eternal beauty of God...the very formless form of the divine loveliness...the heavenly and infinite light, out of time and eternal, the light that makes immortality shine forth, the light which deifies those who contemplate it."

Under the sacred canopy, we see light and we will know love. As Palamas declares, we see the "divine loveliness." In the light we see life; we learn how to live as we learn how to love. The sacred canopy is not solely an individual experience of being in God's presence. It also has a communal character—a gathering of that great people. Eloquently, Thomas Kelly observes that "lives immersed and drowned in God are drowned in love, and know one another in Him, and know one another in love."

As light and love, Jesus walked through the world erecting canopies. He pitched tents of grace. Like a canopy, he stretched out his hands to heal the blind—and they saw. He touched the alienated and lonely—and they loved. His spiritual presence is still spreading over people today. That presence continues to invite us into this graceful tent filled with brilliance and pulsating with energy. His invitation is always and simply, "come in." Come into the canopy of light and love.

Chapter 1
Seasons

Bethlehem Promise

Christmas can be a powerful season—powerful not for economic reasons, but for spiritual reasons. Like sin, however, merchandizing pollutes the spirit of the season. The depth of our Christmas memory only goes back to the last tree or whether it snowed that year! Instead of trees, the genuine Christmas brings the possibility of being free. Christmas is truly the season of freedom.

The fourth century theologian, Gregory of Nazianzus, writes in a Christmas sermon about this powerful freeing season. In the original *Season of Christmas,* the God "who gives riches becomes poor, for He assumes the poverty of my flesh, that I may assume the richness of His Godhead. He that is full empties Himself, for He empties Himself of His glory for a short while, that I may have a share in His fulness."

Near the end of the sermon Gregory adds this exhortation. "Honor little Bethlehem, which hath led thee back to Paradise..." Seasonally understood, Christmas leads us back to paradise—back to our own original, pristine, free relationship with the rich and full God who brought us to birth. By being born as Jesus, God seasonally gives us the possibility of re-birth.

Seen in this light, Christmas is more than an altar call—it is always an *alter* call—a call into a different place and a different way of life. Christmas is the call back into relationship with the creator. Christmas is the experience of engaging our re-creator. The bringing back to paradise—which Bethlehem affords—is, circularly speaking, also a leading forward to the *parousia* (the kingdom). So, Christmas is both *paradise* and *parousia* —both Eden and Kingdom. It represents the beginning and the end—the possibility and the fulfillment.

Gregory beautifully underscores this by saying "today's feast is that of the Theophany (which means "manifestation of God") or the Nativity. It may be called by either name. For God has appeared to us through the Nativity...so that He who first gave us life, now gives us blessed life..." Christmas is the birth of hope, the beginning of blessing and we prepare for Christmas not by shopping, but by stopping! We prepare for the feast of Theophany by stopping our "throw-away" lives. Christmas is the spiritual season to "re-cycle" our lives.

We are offered a clue how to proceed to re-cycle our spiritual lives when we closely examine a portion of a prayer of St. Francis of Assisi which he included at the end of a letter in 1226 A.D. to the entire order of Franciscans. The prayer begins, "Almighty, eternal, just, and merciful God, grant us in our misery (the grace) to do for You alone what we know You want us to do, and always to desire what pleases You." It is in the misery of throwing away our lives that we are given possibility of Christmas grace to recover our desire to please God and to do what the divinity would have us to do. In this grace, Christmas is a call to selflessness rather that the typical seasonal selfishness.

Francis continues the prayer by identifying three movements of the Spirit which *delivers* us into this gracious spiritual season. "Thus, inwardly cleansed, interiorly enlightened, and inflamed by the fire of the Holy Spirit, may we be able to follow in the footprints of Your beloved Son, our Lord Jesus Christ."

We enter the spiritual season by being "inwardly cleansed." This cleansing is best understood as a *purifying* action of God's Spirit on our whole being. Often, it takes the form of detachment. We are inwardly cleansed by stopping the habits and routines which continually alienate us from God and separate us from our neighbors. Purifying knocks the routine of rust from our soul and opens up the spiritual veins through which the blood of Christ pulsates. As we are inwardly cleansed, new life begins to surge through our being.

In addition to feeling new life, we will begin to *know* new life. Francis describes this process as "interiorly enlightened." This reminds us of a much earlier monastic leader, St. Benedict, who began his sixth century *Rule* with these words. "Therefore we intend to establish a school for the Lord's service...(and) as we progress in this way of life and in faith, we shall run on the path of God's commandments, our hearts overflowing with the inexpressible delight of love."

Therefore, in the school of the Spirit we are interiorly enlightened. Enlightenment is more than knowledge; it is the grasp of the "Ah-ha!" Enlightenment is the transformation brought by wisdom. Cleansing makes us vital. Enlightenment makes us bright.

Finally, Francis declares, we are "inflamed by the fire of the Holy Spirit." Because of our purity and brightness, we are now spiritually combustible agents for God's continuing mission in the world. In the secular world Christmas usually follows "trend-setters." In this spiritual season we become "fire-setters!" We are fire-setters because we have been inflamed by the fire of the Holy Spirit.

The fourteenth century English hermit, Richard Rolle, shows how this inflaming process carries us into the joy of the spiritual season. "When Christ grants His favor, the spirit will be marvelously set ablaze to love. Having been burnt, it will be delighted...(and) will praise God in jubilant melody. Indeed, he utters praise to God from his inmost heart and his voice reaches even to the heights with the sweetest song, which the Divine Majesty is delighted to listen to."

Christmas is the spiritual season of melody and delight. Cleansed, enlightened and inflamed—this is what we can "get" in this season. It is the gift of grace—the season for every purpose under heaven. O come, Emanuel, let us celebrate the possibility of your promise!

God's Presence—A Gift

Finally, the Christmas season is here! Christmas has come to be like the NBA professional basketball season—it is so long that when the playoffs come, everyone is already into summer plans; we are "out of season." So when the day of Christmas comes, too often we who have been getting ready for it since October are exhausted by expectation! The early church designed Advent for four weeks; that timing has wisdom.

In October, as the department stores began to energize our western culture with Christmas wares, we simply are not ready. We should still be enjoying Indian summer and emotionally basking in the falling leaves, the pretty colors of red, yellow and brown. It is not time yet for dreaming of a white Christmas and hearing jingle bells throughout our stores. But, think of presents we must—so insists our economic culture.

My favorite department store positions the perfume/cologne display at the foot of the escalator. Effortlessly, the passengers glide from top to bottom—a wondrously mechanized message itself: one does not have to work to get somewhere, the illusion of moving without having to move!

Christmas season begins so effortlessly to sell other illusions—to begin our psychological movement without the feeling of having been moved. Coming down those subtle moving stairs I am introduced into that perfume section. A boldly colored banner proclaims a perfume called "Eternity!" Without the slightest blush to acknowledge that theology is being aped, my store is now selling eternity I am being openly told that eternity can be bought. The banner is telling me that buying "Eternity" will make me smell—divine.

What a Christmas present to offer: Eternity! Who on my list would not want me to give them eternity? I can buy it, have it wrapped and put under my little plastic tree. What a fantastic idea my culture has uncovered: under my plastic tree I can have a gift of eternity for the big day—and eternity will last a day or two! When I come to my senses through this sea of cynicism, I realize my culture actually is right: Christmas is about gifts, presents and eternity. My culture just cannot spell and has not understood.

First, my culture misunderstands gifts: the real gift of Christmas is God through Jesus. "For God so loved the world that he gave his only Son..." (Jn. 3:16) God *gave*. The second cultural misunderstanding is to think it can sell eternity--which only lasts a few days! Rather, through Jesus, God's Christmas gift was for those who, by receiving, become lovers of God. By loving, they receive *eternal* life. Eternal life, according to John, is "that they know thee the only true God and Jesus Christ whom thou hast sent." (Jn. 17:3) Eternity is not perfume, but knowledge of my life in the Spirit. Finally, my culture misspells the real gift of eternity. The gift is not presents but *presence!* God's gift is God's presence.

Christmas celebrates this presence of God. God's present was Jesus and the present still is a *presence* in and with us. We will not find it under our plastic trees, but in each other. Christmas is any day we look and see—give and receive. Christmas happens any day God's gift, Jesus, is discovered. This is no illusion; it is real!

Let's Communicate!

Few among us do not look forward to the daily ritual of the coming of the man or woman bringing the mail. We hurriedly scan the junk mail—all the while looking for those valuable first-class pieces. We quickly sort those into two groups—the uninteresting group like the bills, etc. (always the bigger lot) and the personal (sometimes, sadly, not even one!). When I receive one from the good group, I look at the return address because just knowing who sent it makes a real difference as I open it.

Potentially, letters will become dinosaurs. The telephone has been hard on them; computers are also threatening the personalized, hand-written letter. But, I continue to find letters an appreciated way to say "I care." And to feel care in return almost always happens when I receive a letter.

There are letters and there are letters. By nature I am not a collector of things, but I have a few letters from one whom I counted as a spiritual advisor. He also happened to be a pastor, but for me he was a spiritual friend and, more importantly, a present help when I was cutting my spiritual teeth. A letter from almost twenty years ago still touches me when I read his message of thanks to me. "Your letters always seem to come when I most need a word of love and encouragement...Your new ideas and concepts are also a joy to me—for they reveal that you are willing to encounter, to think, and to change your mind...Just don't come to the place where you feel there is nothing new to learn—for that is fatal."

Letters are a form of communication. Certainly, animals communicate, but humans communicate in special ways and letters are one form of this human communication. Letters use language to say how we feel and what we think and letters disclose to others who we are. Through letters we can know and be known. Letters are *revelations*.

It is an easy step to see that our habits with letters betray our habits with life. We live in a world where there is mass communication, but also massive superficiality. Instead of revelation, we see "cover-up" and I am convinced that those who take seriously the spiritual dimension are also those who can rediscover through letters authenticity in their lives. We can become as one of the Corinthians to whom Paul said, "You yourselves are our letter of recommendation, written on your hearts, to be known and read by all men; and you show that you are a letter from Christ delivered by us, written not with ink, but with the Spirit of the living God, not on tablets of stone, but on tablets of human hearts." (II Cor. 3:2-3)

So, when the postperson comes, hopefully I will have a letter. When the Spirit comes, *be a letter.* As God's epistle, one can go apostolically into the world delivering the good news of God's invitation to friendship. To any who receive you, they will also receive the Spirit of God which is love.

The 'Church' Has Good News!

"If we have not loved and hated, been enriched and injured by others, life has not been lived. For this reason relationships are crucial to our psychological development." These words from John A. Sanford's *Healing and Wholeness* well serve as prefatory words to an understanding of Pentecost. Pentecost is the story of the church's foundation—the church as primary place of relationship between God and people and between person to person. Pentecost necessarily rests on the confessional awareness of who Jesus is. We learn to say with Peter, "You are the Christ, the Son of the living God." (Mt. 16:16) From this awareness, we enter into relationship with the living Christ—as well as with other living Christians.

We join, as it were, those gathered disciples on Easter evening to witness the living Jesus who says once more, "Receive the Holy Spirit. If you forgive the sins of any, they are forgiven; if you retain the sins of any, they are retained." (Jn. 20:22-23) The reception of the Holy Spirit and the gracious power to forgive sins spiritually undergirds the psychological development about which Sanford spoke.

Too often we know too little about Pentecost as a graceful laboratory for relational development. If we see it only as speaking in tongues, we limit our understanding of Pentecost. Rather, the pentecostal account in John's gospel leads us to see the dispensation of the Holy Spirit as the gracious empowering of disciples-in-relationship—empowered to forgive one another. This enables them to learn about life—spiritual life. If Sanford is right, learning about life means knowing about love and hate—being enriched and injured. The church can be the place where such *life-learning* is not only possible but encouraged.

The church is the ongoing manifestation of the living Christ. It is where we who have been inhabited by the Spirit learn to live by *imitatio Christi* — by imitating Christ. It is where we realize that life lived fully brings us love and sometimes provokes hate. Life fully lived incredibly enriches us and sometimes, unfortunately, injures us. Finally, life in the church is where we learn about healing and grow up into wholeness.

The authentically graceful laboratory of life — called the church—does not sell religion between commercials, but shares the good news about a spiritual path to healing and wholeness. In the words of Stephanie Covington and Liana Beckett, authors of *Leaving the Enchanted Forest,* "the spiritual path is a blend of intent and openness to our intuition and unconscious motives, a willingness to trust, a willingness to be tolerant and gentle, a willingness to keep learning from life's lessons." This is why the "pentecostal" church will have to do more work with sinning and forgiving than it does with speaking in tongues. Because the church—at least, when it is pentecostal—is the place where people in relationship are trying to learn how to live and how to love. Again, as Sanford says, "the safe life is not the whole life, and the whole life will have its share of mistakes..." The pentecostal church is that place where disciples can make mistakes—mistakes which come from risking the safe to learn about whole life.

Whole life is not an insurance policy. Rather, it is the promise held out to those willing to enter into relationship with the living Christ and other friends of Jesus. Jesus is not a salesperson, but he does stand at our door and knock. If we open ourselves spiritually, he comes in to form a relationship with us such that life takes on a whole new dimension, a vital new meaning, and it feels like spring-time!

Jesus — Christmas — Love = Gift

In the final analysis, as well as in the first experience, Christmas is about gift. Our commercial culture intuitively knows this truth and explicitly exploits it. Commercially, the danger is that people finally will realize that the only gift of Christmas is love! And love is not for sale — except as a prostitution of the real thing.

Christmas brings the exhilaration of joy and the mire of depression. But, ultimately, it deals with love. With love, there really are only two possibilities: the acceptance of it or the rejection of it. Understanding — or better, experiencing—love in this way always brings humans to a conversion place. As Rosemary Haughton says in *The Passionate God,* "people 'discover' that Christianity is true by a conversion experience, in which they perceive, very simply and directly and without argument, that the revelation of God in Christ is what life is all about."

Christmas, then, is about love—which, in reality, is what life is all about. As a season, Christmas is a chance to interpret ordinary life from the perspective of the *extraordinary.* We humans so frequently are ignorant of the extraordinary (God), that we crash on the rocks of despair or depression, instead of being extraordinarily carried into the deep waters of joy. We tend to keep looking for the extraordinary, but miss it with ordinary eyes. We assume life...and, then, try to figure out something about love.

In fact, the gospel proclaims that there is love and that love creates real life. The good news brings this real breakthrough into our ordinariness. Haughton says that "the Gospels are about life at a point of realness which only needs to be properly seen in order to disclose its meaning and so to create a new world."

The Christmas story then is the story of the creation of a new world. The new world is created by God's passion for human beings; Christmas is the loving God expressed. Christmas contains Easter. In Haughton's words, "Jesus is 'the passionate God' supremely at that moment which turned all of living and loving inside out, which was his death and resurrection." Jesus' Christmas gift is his Easter gift: himself-God! To know Jesus is to know we are loved and to be empowered by that love. And to live!

To have Jesus as passionate God is to have a friend. Haughton tells us that "really to be a friend is to lower one's defences, to be vulnerable to the demands of love." Jesus invites us to be friends at Christmas and, sadly, many would rather have a video! Instead of the video, we all could receive God's letter which personally addresses us and reads, "I love you with my heart and being. You are the passion of my life." What a gift!

Take A Spiritual Vacation

On the surface vacations are great because they alter routine. As we travel to new places, we usually see "strange" things and we visit people with "funny" accents. We observe "odd" ways. But if we reflect on it, suddenly we realize those things we call strange, funny and odd are our designations defined by how *we* see routine.

To go on vacation enables me to become aware that reality can be defined differently through different experiences. Reality both *is* — and also is a matter of *perspective.* Confused? Confusion is always rampant on vacation—but often confusion is the first step of the examined life. Confusion can lead us into a deeper level of awareness. The spiritual journey is like this vacation. In other words, the spiritual "vacation" is to leave our religious home in order to discover a deeper spiritual reality.

Too frequently, we want to make people "religious" instead of encouraging them to develop spiritually. We define religious reality by church attendance or a cultural morality. These are fine and, often enough true, but at another level they may become blocks to a deeper spiritual reality. For this, we need a vacation to go "strange" spiritual places where we will hear "funny" spiritual language and observe "odd" ways of living God's truths. We may never realize how religiously conditioned our reality is until we go on a spiritual vacation. This realization may initially feel like an "unlearning."

Through the words of Don Juan in *Journey to Ixtlan,* Carlos Casteneda speaks to the spiritual pilgrim. "You must erase everything around you until nothing can be taken for granted, until nothing is any longer for sure, for real. Your problem now is that you're too real...You must begin to erase yourself." Jesus invited us to begin erasing. He invited us to take a spiritual vacation. "Follow me," he always beckoned.

And, then, at a deeper spiritual level, he invites us to the school of paradoxical *unlearning* which spiritual vacations teach. "If any person would come after me, let him deny himself and take up his cross and follow me." (Mk. 8:34) Is it any wonder that most of us already assume we know what reality is? We do not need any cross messing up our reality! So we choose—if at all—to be religious, but never to take a spiritual vacation to learn to be spiritual. We stay at home.

But Jesus says, "Follow me." We say, "You go ahead!" And he comes back to begin again. Tenderly, he says, "Come on, now, let's take a vacation."

Live In The Present

We made it through that year—and that year truly was a special one, 1984! George Orwell, we have survived and it was not all like you feared. As we contemplate all those years since—1985 until now and those yet ahead— some of us, if we are old enough, cannot believe "how quickly time passes!" Why, we can remember when Ike—not Reagan or Nixon—won his re-election. Or, some can even remember FDR's re-election! For us, the speed of time's passing is directly related to our age——the older we are, the faster time flies.

And, then, there are those young ones at the other end of the time-line. For them, this current year might bring finally their sixteenth birthday and that "God-given, North American right" to drive a car. For pre-teens time simply moves at a snail's pace. Time does not fly, it lumbers. Everything seems distanced—coming, but never happening. For them, there often is frustration at "how slowly time passes!"

There is a joke going in my circle which says that God created time so that everything would not happen at once! Time does have a way of sorting out, organizing and disciplining what "happens." First, time organizes things in three ways: past, present, and future. For the older person, there is awareness that time has perhaps tipped the scale towards the past. So much *has* happened. The future, while still coming, seems so much less—less promising, less hopeful—sometimes, even threatening. For the older person, the future is bringing their death and that only gets nearer. For the younger person, the time is still tipped promisingly towards the future. For this person, everything is yet to come—so much is possible. Rather than fear of future here, one senses an impatience for the future to come.

What emerges in this stereotype of the older and younger persons is too much concern about what has or has not happened and too little concern about the present. There is a way in which only the aspect of time which is the present is finally worth our concern. Temporally speaking, the present is "like" eternity. Another way of saying this is to suggest that God meets us in our present time. To worry about the past means we miss a divine opportunity in the present. To wait for the future means we have ignored present divine possibilities.

To have time so that not everything can happen at once means we have to choose, but it means we do not have to choose from everything at once. The year 1985 was like 1984—and 2000 will be like 1999—in the sense that God will be "present" for us and to us as God was in 1984. "Now" is a new and renewing chance to *live* in the present.

There is really not life in the past; the past is kept alive only by memory. There is really not life in the future; the future has a life only as hope. There is only life in the present because that is where eternity intersects time—where God meets you and me. We are in the present; let us learn to live in the presence of God's time.

The Beginning Of Transformation

Advent season always leads us to the celebration of Christ's coming. When it is over we look back to see that presents have been exchanged, some expectations have gone unfulfilled and others have been fulfilled. After Christmas there is a way in which life is supposed to return to "normal." This, I think, is the kind of reasoning which early Quakers wanted to avoid when they decided not to celebrate Christmas the way others did. It was a bit like their view of sacraments: Quakers were not against Christmas, but rather against limiting it to one day in the twelfth month.

Quakers never want to leave the reality of Christmas to return to "normal." Christmas is the proclamation and celebration that Jesus Christ is Emanuel ("God is with us") today and tomorrow and forever. To follow Advent is to be brought to a place where that which is "normal" is transformed. When we are transformed by Christmas, we can never return to "normal."

For too many of us, what has been/is "normal" is demanding and seemingly never-ending. To others, "normal" is boredom or, worse, the impending feeling of nothingness or meaninglessness. For yet others, "normal" is pain, suffering and brokenness. Emanuel has stepped into the normalcy of the world and transformed it. Emanuel has been invited into my own personal normalcy and transformed it. To experience this is always my Christmas celebration. In my own case, I can read my journal entry of last July and see that I felt "filled with awe at God's continuing presence…and celebrate this and know that the God who has called me to this place will not abandon me." These words were my recognition of Christmas in July!

Advent is always the invitation to come to Christmas, to know Emanuel—God with you. To know Christmas is to know both the *gift* of God's presence and to accept *responsibility* for that gift. To those of us living in our own demanding, boring, hopeless, painful normalcy Jesus invites us to "come to me, all who labor and are heavy laden, and I will give you rest." (Mt. 11:28) The rest which Jesus gives us is the transformation of our situation. Resting does not mean quitting; it does not even mean that our situation will necessarily change. Resting means that we do not have to be in our situation the way we "normally" are. That is God's gift.

To accept that transforming gift means that we say "yes" to Jesus' request to "take my yoke upon you, and learn from me; for I am gentle and lowly in heart; and you will find rest for your souls. For my yoke is easy, and my burden is light." (Mt. 11:29-30) To be yoked with Jesus is to live in Christmas—to dwell in the presence of God. It is the place to learn what we "normally" will not learn, to be given rest from what we "normally" can never escape.

To be yoked with the Lord is to *be-friended*. We are given direction, support and meaning. In turn, he will send us out looking for "yoke-mates." To him or her we will say, "I have a Christmas gift for you."

Chapter 2
Revelation

In The Image Of God

In his book, *Clowning in Rome,* Henri Nouwen tells the charming story of a little boy watching a sculptor at work on a large block of marble. The boy "saw nothing more than large and small pieces of stone falling away left and right. He had no idea what was happening. But when the boy returned to the studio a few weeks later, he saw to his great surprise a large, powerful lion sitting in the place where the marble had stood. With great excitement the boy ran to the sculptor and said, 'Sir, tell me, how did you know there was a lion in the marble?'"

This little story illustrates the potentiality Jesus, as sculptor of disciples, brings to each of us in his invitation, "Follow me." To follow Jesus means to allow him to start chipping away at our hardness—to begin giving some shape to our rigidities and to bring beauty from our ugliness. The "lion" in us is the "new creature" we each become as we respond to the divine call.

Many of us are too sophisticated even to believe there is a "lion" in us! We are so well-trained to see ourselves and our world as they "really" are that we believe blocks of marble never contain lions—and humans in no way are reflections of divinity. But, a sculptor knows how to bring forth our lion.

The lion in each of us is the *imago Dei,* the image of God, in which each one of us is created. We have it simply because we are human. However, frequently it is so deeply buried in the rockiness of lives squandered or apathetically lived that the image is as hard to see as the lion in the marble. To know we have this image is not a matter of luck. Rather, it is a matter of human destiny because of God's providence in providing an awareness of divinity. In his *Institutes of the Christian Religion* John Calvin, the sixteenth century reformer, acknowledges "there is within the human mind, and indeed by natural instinct, an awareness of divinity *(divinitatis sensum)."*

The image of God is where this *sensus,* this sense or affection, for the divinity lies. This is the connecting point for the divine mystery and the human majesty. The contemporary evangelical theologian, Hendrickus Berkhof in his *Christian Faith,* shows where this human majesty manifests itself. Because we are created in God's image, Berkhof notes, we have "the freedom to love and to exercise power." Berkhof continues, "in creating man, God as it were recedes...to make room for another. That room is needed because the other is to be a partner whom God wants to meet and have fellowship with." By creating us in the divine image, God has "made room" for us. God has given us the choice how we make use of our "room," our space. But, alas, just look at how most of us have done it!

Instead of exercising a freedom to love—to love God and our neighbors—we have learned to hate. We have chosen to fill our space by alienating people—by ostracizing groups unlike us and by destroying possibilities which love offers. Frequently, we are so out of touch with our image of God that, in the words of Nouwen, our real message is "we have to be prepared to live in a world (of) fear, suspicion, mutual distrust, hatred, physical and mental torture..."

Instead of these negative preparations, the call of God in Jesus through the gospel story is the call to exercise our power in another direction. It is an invitation to see the potentiality of a person for another kind of power. In lieu of the oppressive powers of fear, suspicion and hatred- - -

like the baby Jesus who sustained the threat of the Herod- - we can be delivered from the Herods of our world. Jesus—and we—not only survive, but thrive!

Instead of beating a drumbeat of disaster, Jesus introduced a spiritual melody which resonates with the image implanted deep within each of us. We begin to respond to divine music. Jesus is not a Pied Piper. In that story the Pied Piper led rats to a river where they drown and then, because the Piper was not paid, he led the village children to a mountain where they disappeared.

Jesus is not a misleader; he is the musician of our soul. We learn from him the rhythm of life and learn how to overcome the disharmony of oppression and alienation. The nineteenth century German theologian, Friedrich Schleiermacher, says "the virtuosity (or special calling) of a person...is the melody of that person's life, and it remains a simple, meager series of notes unless religion, with its endlessly rich variety, accompanies it with all notes and raises the simple song to a full-voiced, glorious harmony."

Even in the winter season of the soul, there come refreshing, warm breezes of the spirit. The feel of them on our soul causes us to break out in song—to make melody with our lives and to create beauty with our love. As God's melodies, we become God's gifts to the world. We are spiritual lions—sources of amazement to children watching a sculptor at work.

Easter Life

In *Passion for Pilgrimage,* Alan Jones notes that "Easter has largely deteriorated into a secular festival celebrating the coming of spring. At best, it celebrates the cycle of the seasons. At worst, it provides us with yet another occasion to spend money." In order to deal with this deterioration, we do well to back up—back up, so with freshness we can again go forward into Easter.

If we take John's gospel as our cue, this "backing up" can take us to the week before Easter where we read the story of Lazarus. This story represents the culminating sign of the fourth gospel as well as anticipates Jesus' resurrection. The Lazarus story offers us a symbolic chance to learn how to experience Easter. Also, we learn the key to experience Easter is not to focus on Lazarus but focus on Martha. Martha gives us, as readers, the opportunity to discover the spirituality of Easter. As Sandra Schneiders says in a recent article, "spirituality is lived participation in the paschal (Easter) mystery of Christ." Martha is the *active* participant in the Lazarus story.

In addition to Martha, Mary also plays a part in this story. Early in the story both women send for Jesus, informing him, "the one whom you love is ill." (Jn. 11:3) In a somewhat surprising manner, Jesus replies that he loves Martha as well as her sister and Lazarus! (Jn. 11:5) Moving to the Martha section of the chapter (11:17-27), we watch Martha go to meet Jesus as he makes his way to Bethany and the dead Lazarus. She tells Jesus that Lazarus would not have died had Jesus been there, but nevertheless "whatever you ask from God, God will give you." (Jn. 11:22)

This leads to an interchange in which Jesus announces that Lazarus will rise again. Martha misunderstands this to mean at some future time. Jesus then reveals to her: "I am the resurrection and the life; he who believes in me, though he die, yet shall he live, and whoever lives and believes in me shall never die." (Jn. 11:25-26) Here is the amazing revelation of Easter; eternal life is separated from the issue of physical death and is associated with the issue of belief! Jesus offers this life because *he is that life itself.*

By this revealer, Jesus, Martha is confronted with life's question: "Do you believe me?" (Jn. 11:26) She answers with the answer of every believer: "Yes, Lord; I believe that you are the Christ, the Son of God, he who is coming into the world." (Jn. 11:27) There is nothing more to say; the scene ends. For Martha, Easter has begun. Life—real life—has begun.

Martha's scene shows us her answer to life's question is not a doctrinal response but a *transformational* response. Schneider notes "the difference between theology and spirituality is the difference between reflection on revelation and personal commitment to the one who reveals." She adds that Martha's "scene ends abruptly, not because there is something inadequate in Martha's response, but because that response has initiated in her a new life which is the horizon of all further experience." Eloquently, Alan Jones speaks to this new Easter life which is the horizon of all future experience. He says "the resurrection is not, in the first instance, a puzzling doctrine over which to make an intellectual decision. It is an invitation to live and to live *now.*" With this, we have come a long way from chocolate and bunnies!

Easter is not only this story, "Do you believe me," but simultaneously raises the question, "Do you really want to live?" And that question of choosing life is always our asking a question of Jesus. So at Easter—at that horizon of all future experience—we are in the right place to ask, "Do you love me?" Again, Jones sees this "is a question we silently ask all the time. I see it in the eyes of friends and strangers alike. Do you love me? It is a question about resurrection and new life. Our eyes soon glaze over so that the question is hidden once more. Do you love me? This is the question of the Resurrection. Our daring to ask it springs from our longing. Our repressing the question wells up from our terror. It is the question of our yearning dread."

So, the resurrection is both a time of question as well as an occasion for answer. The question always provokes my longing—and expresses my dread. But, Jesus' answer always hooks my hope and touches my fear. The outcome is always clear. To go with dread and fear is, finally, to side with death. Easter is the choice of longing, the gift of life and the satisfaction of love.

Easter is not another Sunday on the threshold of Spring. It is the horizon of eternity—the threshold of vitality. Easter's color should be green, its feel fresh and its face joyous. Easter does have a face: it is the face of Jesus and it is the face of you and me. Easter is the face that elicits my "YES" to life and love.

The Presence In Our Midst.

In 1651 George Fox, the seventeenth century founder of Quakerism, came to the city of Lichfield, England, where he pronounced the famous "Woe." This story is intriguing, less because of what it proclaims, but more for the surrounding context in which it is found. As he approaches Lichfield, George comes into a field where he joins some shepherds. He tells us he was "commanded of the Lord to pull off my shoes of a sudden; and I stood still, and the word of the Lord was like a fire in me."

Mentally we do not have to strain to understand this as a *theophany*. A theopany is an "appearance" of the divine in our midst. The most famous Old Testament theophany is the account of Moses at Horeb, the mountain of God. Fascinating in this story is that Moses himself is a shepherd tending the flock of Jethro, his father-in-law. Coming to Horeb, we are told of Moses that "the angel of the Lord appeared to him in a flame of fire out of the midst of a bush." (Ex. 3:2) Further, we are familiar with the injunction God gave Moses to "put off your shoes from your feet, for the place on which you are standing is holy ground." (Ex. 3:5)

A theophany is the experience of encountering God—and realizing we are in a "holy place." We see and feel things and respond appropriately (albeit "weirdly" in the eyes of the world). In Fox's case at Lichfield, he received a mission to go into the city and cry "Woe unto the bloody city of Lichfield." In beautiful Quaker language George narrates, "when I had declared what was upon me and cleared myself, I came out of the town in peace about a mile to the shepherds." Comically, George buys his own shoes back but, as he recounts, "the fire of the Lord was so in my feet and all over me that I did not matter to put my shoes on any more and was at a stand whether I should or no till I felt freedom from the Lord so to do." It mattered not that it was Winter; he was in God's presence!

Theophanies are not limited only to the biblical or historical; they still occur. I have friends who have felt the fire of the Lord burn in their hearts and within their inner being. They have known God and were led to a holy place. Their obedience has less to do with shoes than with life. Like Fox, those of us who have come to know God's fire will be called to *reach* out and *go* out. Frequently, the call will not be a woe but "come."

Come to the warmth of God's fire; come to know this healing presence for yourself. To have God's fire may make those around us uncomfortable. We may be seen as abnormal, unusual, provocative. But all people who are chilled need warmth, the lonely need a friend and the destroyed need healing. As God's firepersons, we need to go to the fire, share it and, then, go out into the world and set holy fires!

Is There More?

The person who has experienced God's Spirit is convinced of a level of reality beyond or behind the surface reality of this world as we all know it. This deeper, invisible reality we associate with God. Classical theologians tell us that God is not knowable in God's own nature; that would be to know God in God's own divine essence and we would have to be divine to know this. Rather, we know this divine level or reality only insofar as that reality is revealed unto us.

Revelation is seen as a glimpse; it comes as a hint; we know it in passing and as process. We know the divinity not so much as life, but more as vitality. We learn about God not from sight as much as from insight—that is, from our perception. To know God is never to be able to prove God, but only to be able to witness to God's reality. Langdon Gilkey in his book, *Message and Existence,* captures this flow by declaring that revelation "means the communication of the divine *power* (being, life, health, and eternal life), of the divine *truth* (order, illumination, insight, and meaning), and of the divine *love* (mercy, forgiveness, and renewing, reuniting, *love*)."

In our scientific age it is rather easy to conclude that this world and our "seen" reality is all there is. To talk about another level of reality beyond this present "real" world is dismissed as illusory. Every one of us who knows and feels something about this deeper level of reality necessarily bears some caution in distinguishing between illusion and hope. In her book, *Beyond God the Father,* Mary Daly has commented that "our planet is inhabited by half-crazed creatures, but there is consistency in the madness." I have suspected that all of us are mad in some way. Those of us who choose the spiritual—or, perhaps, sense in some way we have been chosen by the Spirit—know and feel our madness because we have chosen that "illusion" which others claim does not even exist. Who can really know?

Out of my own experience of that other, deeper divine reality I feel confident about a hope. Without that divine reality, I fear I would finally feel that this world and this reality in which I live would be meaningless. To be meaningless does not mean that this world would be uninteresting. In fact, that is the illusion of thinking there is only this world: it is so interesting—partly because we have created it in our own image!

At the end of the twentieth century in the Western world this interesting world is also amazingly complex. The illusion—and the tragedy— however, is the assumption that interesting is synonymous with meaningful. But, it is just at this juncture of interest and meaning that we find the world's reality capable of showing a deeper level which will reveal the resource of hope. This is the place where God is revealed—a place where no human question is left unanswered and where no authentic human desire is unmet.

God's radical act of madness was to become human—just to be our friend! It happened "normally" in an out-of-the-way place in our world. The divine invitation to friendship is about as real as it can be. Don't fall into the trap of our culture seeing this as "corny." Rather, fall in love instead!

Words And The Word

"Have a nice day," the store clerk snarled. Clearly, she was not having a nice day! I have grown to dislike that phrase—not because I am against nice days, but because so often it does not feel "real." It is so overused; indeed, it often feels abusive. I think most people who wish "nice days" to me could not care less how my day goes. As I leave the store having been wished a nice day, I pass folks who will recognize me and in passing ask, "How are you?" If they wanted to know how I am, I would have to wheel around, catch up and begin to tell them. I think about the times I have asked that question without the slightest desire or intention to provide space for the person to tell me. I use an expression of concern to express my not caring!

I have an intrigue about language. I appreciate the power of language, but also am troubled by its abusive superficiality and ability to mislead. Language is beautiful because it is so human. Not one of us is born talking. We gurgle, groan, cry and babble; we do not talk. As adults, we know the linguistic potentiality in the noisy infant. We know that the development of the power of language is related to the development of the brain. What a miracle!

But language is also communal. Language gives us a clear window to the mental, emotional and psychic world of another human being. We are able to say what we think, describe how we feel and paint a verbal picture of our soul's disposition. In dialogue with another person my words are *revelation*. By sharing words about myself, I am sharing myself. Communication is revelational. I can disclose *who* I am by what I say. Revelation is a "making known" or "visible" that which is unknown or hidden. This represents the power of the word: to reveal.

When someone asks me how I am, but waits not for my response, their words are mis-leading. They have used the means to lead to revelation, but by their action say "I really do not want to know!" There is a discrepancy between what they have asked and their unwillingness to receive what they have asked. This suggests that language has also a "negative" power—a power to deny, to conceal and to destroy relationship. It has the power to conceal rather than reveal. By language I can "appear" to care and not care at all. With language I have the ability to communicate nonsense!

It is not a surprising jump to realize that a discussion of words can lead to an awareness of the Word. As Christians, we are aware that the Word of God is the expression of the divine Being in our world. The Word, as John's gospel describes, is both with God and from God. As God's expression, the Word is revelatory. The word speaks God's mind. When in Jesus the Word became human, people everywhere and for all time were given a clear and concrete expression of God's care for the divine creation.

We recognize how and why Jesus' life "spoke" to his friends and "speaks" to us as his friends. When Jesus called his friends to himself, he showed them the way and truth and gave them life. He communicated with them—and to them communicated this abundant life. When we know this life, we, too, can begin to communicate it to others and "speak" vitally. That truly will be to offer them "a nice day!"

Jesus As Flesh And Fresh.

During a recent preaching engagement I made one of those funny slips of the tongue. I was wanting to make a point about God's work in Jesus and intended to quote the incarnational passage from John's gospel, "and the Word became flesh." (Jn. 1:14) As I proclaimed God's special presence in Jesus, my mind was running ahead of my mouth. With proper seriousness I said, "and the Word became *fresh*." Everyone chuckled at the "flesh" which had become "fresh!"

We Christians claim God's unique—and fresh—presence in Jesus as the Word become flesh. God's incarnation is a very particular, concrete way God became involved in the world. With the Jews, we have shared the proclamation that God has always been actively present in history—first, as creator and, then, as sustainer. God has called out a people, related to them through a special covenant, rebuked them when they went wrong and cared for them in their restoration. And yet, God preferred a more universal and personal means to speak to all humankind. By choosing actually to come in the flesh, God indeed chose a "fresh" way to relate to the world and the people for whom God cares. As John's gospel puts it, "God so loved the world that he gave his only Son." (Jn. 3:16)

I have often described God's work in and through Jesus as novel or unique. I have tried to portray the "extra-ordinariness" of this divine participation in human nature. What had never occurred to me was the "freshness" of this divine approach. The Old Testament is full of different ways God appeared to men and women. Never did God become flesh. To become flesh was a *fresh* way to do it! It is a fresh way because in Jesus one could actually "see God;" through Jesus' words one could "hear God;" as Jesus heals, one could "touch God." What a lucky break for those living in Jesus' time—to see God's fresh approach.

However, it dawns upon me to suggest that we still live in Jesus' time—the "living Christ" is still present. As Holy Spirit—who is the living Christ today—God still encounters us. In this we can begin to realize how God is yet fresh. God still comes into flesh, in my flesh and your flesh. Insofar as that spiritual experience moves us as Christians to witness in the world, we have become God's "fresh" participation in the world.

As people met Jesus and saw God, so do we Christians afford our contemporaries a chance to look at us and "see, hear and touch God." What a challenge, what a privilege! With this mission how can Christians become stale or lifeless? We must stay alive, stay fresh in order that the "Word can become fresh" in the lives of our friends around the world.

Christmas—The Beginning Of Easter

Who is this Jesus? A first-born son of Mary wrapped in swaddling cloths in a manger...or a middle-age political revolutionary who met an untimely death by crucifixion at the hands of the Romans...or the proclaimed Lord who is experienced in a resurrected, living fashion by disciples of the first century and the twentieth century?

The Christmas season celebrates the first of these figures of Jesus. We see live nativity scenes played with real babies and braying donkeys. We will see our own children put on silly looking cotton to be funny looking sheep. We will watch a daughter try to keep flimsy wings in place and a halo straight in order more convincingly to be angelic! As serious Christians, we will inevitably experience mixed emotions between our faith and the commercialism of the "Christian" American culture which in December can be oppressive. Somehow, we lament the all too easy transition from the baby wrapped in swaddling cloths to the "real life" baby who wets in her diaper or an 1984 model of Cabbage Patch dolls.

On its own in American culture, the Christmas season always runs the risk of being taken over by our secular impulses. Too many people confuse God's Spirit with Jack Daniels! There is pressure to have fun and to be happy. "Merry" Christmas is the greeting which passes our lips—often without thought- - - as we might say to a crying, broken person, "have a good day!" For too many of us the Christmas party will once more take place in the Hilton; we will be unaware of a couple with a baby "outside" in the manger.

In order to find Christmas—Jesus, the baby—we will have to recall the other figures of Jesus. Again, we will have to remember the political revolutionary who talked about another kingdom than the Roman empire. Again, we will have to hear of the killing of that Jesus who taught disturbing things about peace and joy of this divine kingdom and offered women and men hope for a meaningful life with God. Most importantly, we will have to rehearse the life-transforming event of that Jesus' resurrection and the "rebirth" which that resurrection offers men and women.

Easter, then, really is the beginning of the Christmas story. Christmas only receives meaning in light of Easter. The commemoration of the birth of Jesus is different than tilting angel wings and straying sheep. Christmas is not a holiday from work. Christmas is an encounter with the God "Who was, and Who is, and Who is to come." The ultimate symbol of Christmas is not a green tree but a cross! The gift of Christmas is not a baby "true to life," but life itself.

We do well to "celebrate" Christmas through this resurrection lens. In *Passion for Pilgrimage* Alan Jones writes "the Resurrection is not, in the first instance, a puzzling doctrine over which to make an intellectual decision. It is an invitation to live and to live *now.*" Christmas is the season to join together as friends of Jesus and celebrate our life together. We need not say "Merry Christmas;" rather something like "go for it!"

Chapter 3
Wisdom

Look For The 'Want To'

I have just experienced the joy of watching my second daughter, Christina learn to ride a bicycle. It has taken too long in preparation! We began the summer she was three—because her six year old sister could! To a three old you don't say, "You can't." You simply let them *learn* they can't! Last summer at age four we came close. My wife—being the mechanic of our family—took off the training wheels. Periodically, my wife and I took turns running along—bent backs and creaking legs—trying to assist the avoidance of disaster. In spite of our good words of encouragement, there was little basis for hope. Christina wobbled—as if drugged. Fortunately, we knew she was not inept—*simply not ready.*

And now she is five. Today she came home from a friend's house and excitedly announced she had learned to ride a "two-wheeler!" Her parents had mixed feelings—for two summers we have sacrificed backs, muscles and nerves to give her aspirations room to develop. Nothing... Then, she goes to a friend's house and in one afternoon with a six year old rides a bike! How did we know she was going to wake up on a Tuesday and suddenly be *ready?*

As I ponder these events, two things hit me. How did she know she was ready? I can well imagine she did not know she was until presented with an *opportunity.* Given a chance, she tried and suddenly discovered she was ready and away she rode! I know more about the Spirit than I do teaching bicycle-riding, but there must be similarities. There is a "ripe" time for us to move into new spiritual places.

Two things are necessary for this movement to happen. We have to have the *desire*—the "want to"—to see movement happen. Secondly, we have to have an *opportunity*—a chance—to step into new life, deeper life, fuller life with God. Generally, people are not inept; they just are not ready. Either they do not spiritually want to move into a deeper place or they see no opportunity for new movement.

A second observation to note is my daughter learned to ride with a friend. Someone who was near and wanted to help assisted her into this new, adolescent phase of life. Someone whom she calls a friend has given her the ability more quickly to range much farther from home. A spiritual friend is like that. She or he is someone who can assist us to "get going" by saying, "Come on, you *can* do it."

Those of us who already are "spiritual riders" need to be on the lookout for any "spiritual youngsters" who can not yet ride. We need always to be alert to some potential readiness. With courage and with encouragement we can walk up and say, "Want to learn how to ride?"

Experience Life

In one of his Lake Wobegone stories Garrison Keillor tells about Dale, a young high school graduate who decides to join the Navy. The point is less that Dale joins the Navy, than he epitomizes the "seizing of the day." Through Dale, Keillor is able to show how to embrace life—to form our future—and not to squander our future on useless endeavors. Dale does not represent youth—he represent "possibility." More powerfully, Dale actualizes his possibility—he lives.

In a moving scene Dale is sitting in an algebra class taking an examination when he is caught up with his imaginative possibility. At that moment he chooses life. Dale comments, "life is so wonderful that it is all we can do simply to experience it, and all the things people think are important—none of it matters if it makes us less able to live." Dale's story is told to help us be more "able to live."

For centuries the Christian church has shared *hagiography* (which means stories of holy women and men)—stories to model the spiritual life and to challenge us into it. Hagiography is more than biography. A biography simply narrates the life of a person—her chronology, her thoughts, deeds and meaning. Biographies can be about famous people like Churchill or lesser known folks. But, hagiography moves biography in the direction of the holy (the *hagios*). Hagiography explores and explains how the Spirit moves into biography and begins a sanctifying process. Spiritually, hagiography tells us something we know and shows us something we can be.

Hagiography is the most important kind of story-telling the church can do. Newspapers do "human interest" stories; the church should do "divine interest" stories! One such contemporary divine interest story is Thomas Merton (1915-1968). He is a fascinating divine interest story because of his pilgrimage—an intellectual pilgrimage through non-faith to faith. His pilgrimage carried him through sin to sanctity—but he was not a domesticated saint! Merton became famous as a monk, but was a pain for the abbot of his monastery. His life is hagiography because he reflects our century, our problems and our possibilities—indeed, what makes us "able to live."

In her biography, *Merton*, Monica Furlong captures the essential understanding of Merton-the-saint-in-process when he is visited at the monastery by an old friend. The exchange unfolds. "'Tom...you haven't changed at all.' 'Why should I? Here,' he said, 'our duty is to be more ourselves, not less.'" Being more himself, he was "able to live."

Merton wanted to be free, but learned through painful experience that in his story this freedom demanded that God be present. In his biography, *Thomas Merton: Brother Monk*, Basil Pennington says "Tom had come to know the need of something beyond, something that can free one even from death. Otherwise, all freedom would be illusory and, even in the longest of lives, short lived." For Merton "the Christian is the one who has 'decided for' the Parousia, for the final coming of the Kingdom.' His whole life was oriented by this decision. He prayed, 'Thy Kingdom come!'"

To decide for the kingdom freed him and frees us to live—ourselves to become "divine interest" stories. Our biographies are permeated with God's Spirit and those biographies are re-written as hagiographies—as holy stories. Pennington notes that "in our freedom lies our greatest dignity; therein we image God. This is so because in our freedom lies our power to love, and God is love." Here lies the key to hagiography—holy story-telling. It is the power to love—to love God, to love ourselves and to love others.

This is where Dale—who wants to be "able to live"—has not yet learned what Merton knew. Merton knew *the power to love*—to love because you know God is love. Going to the Navy will not do that—at best, the Navy produces human interest stories. Going to God will lead to love because going to God is going to the love story itself. Knowing this love story is knowing that God always actualizes the power to love AND the power to live. The power to live is abundant living—such that it "spills over" into others' lives and sanctifies them with the power of your own divine interest story.

The familiar nineteenth century hymn, "I Love to Tell the Story," recounts the divine love story. Jesus is the foundational aspect of God's love story—the divine power to love. This power is incarnate in Jesus and spills over into his followers. In time this gospel love story became "legend." Many followers developed a "saga" of their own. Some, like Francis of Assisi, were "fabled" everywhere.

As long as the divine Spirit blows afresh, the divine love story will be told and new stories created. These stories always are fresh. There is no fiction, but faith—faith leading to fraternity. Publishers of truth from this storied community will continue to go forth into a world hungry for news. They will tell of good news—the good news will be a simple story: finally, all are "able to live."

We Hear, But Do We Listen?

"In a certain sense, every single human soul has more meaning and value than the whole of history with its emptiness, its wars and revolutions, its blossoming and fading civilization." These words from Nicholas Berdyaev, *The Fate of Man in the Modern World*, articulate what many of us would like to feel but do not—namely, that we matter and count. Instead, frequently we are left feeling insignificant and meaningless.

We are glad Berdyaev thinks our soul has meaning and value—but, we feel more the sentiments expressed by Gerald May in his book, *Simply Sane*. Instead of meaning and value, we feel alienated from ourselves and our world. May says, "alienation is a wandering emptiness, dry, lifeless, barren. There is a quality of quiet to the despair of alienation." We need some sound to break this quiet, a new song to dispel the despair. The gospel story makes this sound and sings the new song. Fresh winds of God's Spirit carry this sound and bear this new song with their breezes.

The fresh winds of the Spirit connect when our quiet cries are heard. And we sense the fresh winds of the Spirit when someone speaks a word to us—when we are personally and invitationally addressed. Too often, we live impersonally in a barren world which bosses us around saying, "Hey you, do this...be that...think thus." Our soul longs for someone to say "My friend" instead of "Hey you."

Indeed, there is someone who can hear me, know my inner desire and address me as friend. God can and through Jesus does. The Psalmist wrote, "I waited patiently for the Lord; he inclined to me and heard my cry." (Ps. 40:1) That Psalm continues by noting God "drew me up from the desolate pit, out of the miry bog." (Ps. 40:2) To be delivered from the desolate pit of alienation is to be placed where the fresh winds of the Spirit are blowing.

All too often, our ears have ceased to be attuned to the sounds of divinity. That same Psalm has a wonderful metaphor for learning to listen. Acknowledging that God has no desire for sacrifice and offerings, the Psalmist declares "Thou hast given me an open ear." (Ps. 40:6) This RSV translation has lost the power of the metaphor. The Hebrew more accurately is translated, "ears thou hast dug for me." God digs ears so we can hear God's word and "take it in."

In his book, *Working the Angles*, Eugene Peterson perceptively plays with this image of God opening us by digging ears. "Imagine a human head with no ears. A blockhead. Eyes, nose, and mouth, but no ears. Where ears are usually found there is only a smooth, impenetrable surface, granitic bone. God speaks. No response. The metaphor occurs in the context of a bustling religious activity deaf to the voice of God." We who are trapped in our alienation are spiritual blockheads! We are like humans with no ears. Oh, we have physical ears which function to take in sound waves so we have access to a world—but it is a world of noise, what Peterson calls "garbage chatter." It is a world of alienation instead of harmony. God has digging to do.

Peterson tells us how God is present and ready to dig. "God is speaking and must be listened to. But what good is a speaking God without listening human ears? So God gets a pick and shovel and digs through the cranial granite, opening a passage that will give access to the interior depths, into the mind and heart." This work of God is an "opening" work.

Through our newly dug ears God can speak the word which penetrates our minds and comes in to touch our hearts. With these new ears allowing God access to our inner person—our very heart and soul—we are known. Insofar as we are known, we are loved. In this sense, hearing leads to loving. Listening is an act of love. Loving overcomes our alienation.

The intimacy of listening displaces the emptiness of alienation. God's fresh rain of speaking breaks up our dry, lifeless soil and prepares our soul to bear the fruits of the Spirit. In these fruits are found the value and meaning which make every single human soul more important than the whole of history.

The discovery of our self-importance and the acceptance of God's love comes through the gift of dug ears—ears opened by the gentle touch of divinity. A practical spirituality clues us and others how to cultivate the possibilities of open ears. The first point of this practical spirituality came with the beginning of the Psalmist's word: *waiting* patiently for the Lord. (Ps. 40:1) In this sense, God is like a divine train! Stop, look and listen.

Secondly, we who listen will get a *gift*—a gift of song. The Psalmist assures us when we wait, we will hear God—God will "put a new song in my mouth." (Ps. 40:3) Instead of crying, we will start singing. Instead of the quiet of alienation, we will fill the air with the music of incorporation.

Thirdly, our song will have *content.* Once more, in the words of the Psalmist, the content is "the glad news of deliverance." (Ps. 40:9) The hills really are alive with the sound of music. But, the gospel's glad news of deliverance is much more than a famous musical. It is the conviction and confidence that our human souls have value and meaning.

Let the show go on!

Look For Living Movements

In his nineteenth century spiritual classic, *Apologia Pro Vita Sua*, the Anglican-turned Catholic, John Henry Newman, comments on the nineteenth century Oxford Movement in England: "Living movements do not come out of committees.." Indeed, for too many in the Christian movement it seems as if "movement" stops when committees begin! In too many cases committees have become the scene of studied inactivity. Institutionally, we always know when someone has "made it" when that person is appointed to committee.

Religious movements apparently have a built-in drive towards institutionalism. Institutional mechanisms develop for group identity and, consequently, harden for group survival. For example, in the Quaker movement this development came about with the local and yearly meeting organization. Committees arose as means to conduct our life together. But, too often, we have confused the life of the community with the life of a committee! Committees are appropriate for focusing the direction of community movement in the Spirit. They can be channels for the Spirit's work in people's lives. Committees are always effective as *responses* to God's spiritual movement.

Committees who are responding to spiritual movement are typically "responsible." They embody a vitality because the committee members sense the Spirit moving. These committees pulsate with energy because of this movement. It feels like folks are going somewhere, doing something. Because of God's movement, there is an investment and importance in this gathering.

Newman's quotation, however, reminds Christians what we too painfully know—on their own, committees do not produce living movements. When committees begin to run independently of God's Spirit, the committee becomes a fossil—a living reminder of what once was. It is amazing how many committees spend energies maintaining museums!   As fossils, we enshrine the past in a kind of "living museum" where we all have bit parts.

Committees tend toward irresponsibility because they take on a life of their own rather than living the life of the Spirit. Rather than respond to the Spirit's movement, committees begin to manage and, then, control the movement. When committees take control, then clearly the institution is "set" and the spiritual movement is threatened. At this level, the irresponsibility of a committee results in a condemnation to irrelevancy. One goes to a meeting to observe life-less people conducting irrelevant business.

Living movements come out of living members! We are living members insofar as we have come to be in the body of Christ. It is in the body—and as the body—that we gather to hear Jesus' call to life and life abundantly. It is in and as this body we know the God in whom "we live and move and have our being." (Acts 17:28) Authentic life in this body produces living movements—primitive Christianity, early Quakerism, vibrant Methodism—and anybody else who is committed to following the bliss of Jesus.

Frequently, we the committed become the "committee-d". Instead of movement, we mediate between competing institutional interests. Instead of being led by a sense of the meeting, the committee is misled by the non-sense of irrelevancy.

At this point, we do well to remember that Jesus came not to call committees. Rather, he came and called people into friendship. He did not move into people's lives and say, "Let's meet." Rather, his inviting words were, "Let's be friends. Let's go. Let's move."

And We Again Murmur

When fresh winds of the divine Spirit blow into our lives, they are not always received with gratitude or delight. Often, God's Spirit feels disruptive and sometimes dislocates us. Frequently, we are brought to complain rather than celebration. This leads us to acknowledge what can be called the "theology of murmuring,"—a theology which carries a sub-title, "an exploration of the spiritual dysfunction of grumpiness."

Murmuring has a long history in religious traditions! Upon close examination, we discover murmuring generally plays a negative role in the lives of individuals and groups. Unfortunately, murmuring is not just a historical phenomenon; there is evidence everywhere today of much spiritual grumpiness! By understanding it, we have a better chance to see how God can transform murmuring into ministry.

The first characteristic of murmuring is its wilderness association. After God liberated the Israelites from the bondage of Egypt, Moses led them into the wilderness. For three days they were in the wilderness of Shur with no water. They came to Marah, a body of water, but it was undrinkable because it was bitter. Now, the murmuring begins! The Israelites start to murmur against Moses and "he cried to the Lord; and the Lord showed him a tree, and he threw it into the water, and the water became sweet." (Ex. 15:24)

This story shows an important feature of murmuring. Frequently, when God's fresh winds begin to blow, we expect a miracle—but we want the privilege of defining the miraculous! To be in the wilderness causes us to murmur and we want a miracle—we want out. If the miracle does not immediately deliver us, we complain and decide to go back to Egypt. We are ready to ditch the divine project of the promised land and return to the stale bondage.

Honestly, many of us probably do not expect a miracle—but we hope for something magical. We just magically want to get out of the wilderness—because the wilderness is where usually we are more distressed, more uncomfortable and more uneasy. The trouble with murmuring is it changes nothing: magic never does—because magic is not real. God gave the Israelites a miracle: sweet water—water which enabled them to continue the journey.

To go back to Egypt is to let the murmuring "win"—which is really to lose. It is a choice for the numbness of slavery to the fresh winds of freedom. To go back is to kill the awareness which is necessary for freedom. In his book, *Simply Sane,* Gerald May comments

> Immediate awareness is killed in countless ways; in work, in play, in human relationships, in food, in worry, in racing toward success. It is no accident that one says 'I lost myself,' to describe the drowning of awareness in activity. Dulled, robotic, moving through life oblivious to being, we awaken to immediate living only now and then. And most of those precious waking moments become caught up in the evaluation of the past or worry about the future. But it is not really our 'self' which is lost in the daze of doing. It is awareness. Awareness is killed.

The wilderness always brings awareness to the surface and this often brings the murmuring which is a process of slow killing.

It is noteworthy to look at the Israelites murmur against Moses. In another place Moses and Aaron both "get" it: "you have brought us out into this wilderness to kill this whole assembly with hunger." (Ex. 16:3) To this murmuring, God again responds with a miracle: the manna. This story of complaining shows a second characteristic of the theology of murmuring. Murmuring grows out of discontent—which is usually grounded in anger.

When we murmur, we are usually mad at somebody or something for our state or condition. We can even be mad at ourselves. The problem is not the anger; anger is a normal emotion which can be experienced and expressed in healthy ways. Murmuring is an unhealthy anger—usually expressed in a continuous grumpy way, a muted muttering about the one who traps us in our state. Unlike healthy anger, murmuring is picky, petty and continually unsettling. It is often so "soft" no one can hear well enough to deal with it. In this sense, murmuring is always insidious.

This feature of murmuring brings another observation. Murmuring is an unhealthy complaining that attempts to "get" the person who "got" us. That is to say, I will make them responsible for my predicament and, then, punish them by making their lives miserable like mine is miserable! We can even do this to ourselves. I "get" them by making them a "loser."

Murmuring is the chronic annihilation of life. It is a cancer to God's fresh winds of the Spirit. Murmuring is my non-receptive mode to the presence of God's kingdom, the promise of life. Murmuring is complaining about the way things are—the way I am—without any sign of hope for what could be. Murmuring destroys hope and ridicules joy.

As the Exodus story shows, it is exactly at the place of bitterness that God delivers sweetness. The miracle is not to remain in bitterness or go back to it, but to let fresh trees fall into our stale and bitter water. Also, the Exodus story shows at the place of hunger God delivers plenty. Those who murmur because they are feeling deprived—or hoard because they are afraid there is not enough—can relax: there is so much everyone will be filled—filled with love and joy.

So, what are we murmurers complaining about? There will be no murmuring in the kingdom! Why do we hear so much murmuring now? Even in the church? The good news is God's fresh winds are blowing. There is no reason to buy a round-trip ticket when God leads us out of Egypt. The stop-over in the wilderness can be a source of amazement, not murmuring. Let's celebrate!

Where Is My Heart
Where Is My Home

In the well-known prophecy to Laodicea Jesus says, "behold, I stand at the door and knock; if any one hears my voice and opens the door, I will come in to him and eat with him, and he with me." (Rev. 3:20) In this scene Jesus is using imagery from the Old Testament Wisdom tradition. In the Wisdom tradition the "door" is the metaphor by which we enter into that place where God's Wisdom is—or through which that Wisdom enters the heart of a person.

Proverbs tells us Wisdom builds a house. She sends out her maids to call us. "Whoever is simple, let him turn in here." (Prov. 9:4) Further, Wisdom invites us to dine with her: "come, eat of my bread and drink of the wine I have mixed." (Prov. 9:5) Indeed, in this Wisdom tradition the spiritual journey is described as coming to *know*— to know Wisdom as God's presence and ourselves as students of Wisdom. In the Old Testament Apocrypha we read "Wisdom is bright and unfading, and she is easily seen by those who love her, and found by those who search for her." (Wis. of Sol. 6:12) To begin the spiritual journey in pursuit of Wisdom is to desire instruction from the One who will teach us to love— and, further, "the desire for wisdom leads to kingdom." (Wis. of Sol. 6:20)

Jesus, as one who incarnated Wisdom, also leads us by instruction. He teaches us to know love and leads us into a kingdom. But, what does it look like in our contemporary world? In his powerful book, *The Road to Daybreak*, Henri Nouwen tells a story with similar Jesus-Wisdom motifs. Nouwen was still teaching at Yale when a woman, Jan Risse, rang his doorbell. She was there to bring greetings from Jean Vanier, founder of the L'Arche communities for mentally handicapped people.

With a bit of exasperation, Nouwen says he could not believe she only wanted to bring greetings; she must want something else! "No, no," she says, "I just came to bring you greetings from Jean!" Finally, Nouwen invites her into his apartment to spend the day in retreat while he is off being "busy." Nouwen comes home to a beautifully set dinner—table with food, flowers and friendship—all fixed with ingredients Nouwen already had in his house. Stunned, Nouwen comments, "it then dawned on me that something unique was happening. A stranger had walked into my home and, without asking me for anything, was showing me my own house."

Metaphorically, the stranger who walks into our hearts (home) to show us truly who we are—whom we can become—is always God's representative—or better, God's angel. Whether it is a woman we thought we knew—or Wisdom—or Jesus—the experience is always revelatory. We are shown the sacred within us. We are invited to the spiritual banquet at our Center. There we are nourished, nurtured and loved. In this experience the stranger always turns out to be a friend. This friend comes to my door with an offer of life—abundant life. Open your heart and learn!

God Wants To Tent With Us

We live in an age of ad hoc spirituality! We run *to this* and, we run away from that *to this* over here. In Latin "ad hoc" means "to this." Spiritually speaking, ad hoc characterizes a people who often become disappointed with various self-help books, but who are still seeking meaning in their lives. Ad hoc spiritual enthusiasts run to the next promise of fulfillment; they often crash on the foolishness of fads.

In American culture—if not Western culture in general—our own way of life is symbolized by space rather than depth. We still are intrigued by the "wide open spaces"—spaces mythically painting a story of the wild west. We are artificially titillated by the "contemporary" wild west through "Miami Vice" or "L.A. Law". Then, effectively sedated by this superficiality, we lumber from the safety of our easy chair to the rolling comfort of our water beds.

Depth is measured by the exposure of the soul's roots to a God who called people into a desert to make them a divine people. These people followed a God who "tented" among them. In an incredibly radical way, this God "tented" among us by becoming flesh. "The Word became flesh and dwelt (*skeneo*) among us." (Jn. 1:14) This Greek term, *skeneo*, "to live in a tent," reflects the Old Testament sense of God's presence with the people and, more radically, the New Testament sense of God's dwelling *as person* on earth in Jesus. Contemporarily, God is still tenting with us by spiritually "inhabiting" us.

This divine inhabitation is what spirituality is all about. Sadly, ad hoc spirituality is not a concern with divine inhabitation—with God in Christ coming to live in us. Ad hoc spirituality is more like a weekend fling with the divine—a frivolous flirtation designed for kicks but not for keeps. Ad hoc spiritualities are like weekend camping trips when God's "tenting" is pre-conditioned by a not too modest recreation vehicle (RV) with all the guarantees of home and happiness!

Hildegard of Bingen, twelfth century German Benedictine saint, tells us our *soul* is the tent. But, for too many of us, a tent is a lousy, flimsy and long-term uncomfortably inadequate image for our soul. Instead, we have lived our souls into the hardness of stone. We are now committed to this stony place instead of the happy spaciousness of God's place. We are no longer free.

To be truly happy means we truly have to be free. And truly to be free means we will truly be ourselves. In Merton's novel, *My Argument With the Gestapo*, he has the main character say, "If you want to identify me, ask me not where I live...but ask me what I think I am living for...and ask me what I think is keeping me from living fully the thing I want to live for. Between these two answers you can determine the identity of any person. The better answer he has, the more of a person he is."

Jesus was fully a person because in his soul God completely tented—God was completely present and filled his soul with the divine Spirit. For me to become full means opening my soul to God, allowing God through Jesus to come into this stony soul and begin softening. This softening is the process of truly learning what is worth living for—and to overcome that which prevents me from having it. I want God and God wants me.

"What is our life on earth, if not discovering, being conscious of, penetrating, contemplating, accepting, loving this mystery of God's, the unique reality which surrounds us, and in which we are immersed like meteorites in space?" These words in Carlo Carretto's book, *Letters from the Desert*, offer an intriguing way to understand our life in God's spacious environment. We are like meteorites in space. A meteorite occupies a place in space, but space is infinitely larger than any particular meteorite's place. In fact, space is so vast a single meteorite could be overwhelmed.

And so it is with our life on earth. If we stop ourselves long enough to become aware of who we are and where we are, we run the risk of being overwhelmed. We can be overwhelmed by our insignificance, our emptiness, our loneliness, our mortality. We could feel like a fatalistic meteorite—careening through space towards the inevitable crash of death.

Only if we can understand this vast space of earth and beyond as God's, can we transform this feeling of being overwhelmed into one of overcoming. In that way, life could be seen as an invitation to become a spiritual astronaut. The spiritual astronaut prepares for a life of adventure. Carretto has already given us the life-map for our trip—the goal of which is to be brought to a place of loving this mystery of God. For a spiritual astronaut to come to this place is always a blast. To begin requires a blast off!

Discover Life

Following Carretto's lead, we understand that our spiritual life on earth is first of all *discovery*. It is discovery that we are not alone—careening through our own personal universe. Discovery is an awakening to what is already there; it is the emergent awareness of one's situation. Discovery is not yet knowing—but it is to be in a place where the learning can come and the knowing take root. Without this discovery of God's mystery in our very midst, we can do nothing but exist in a fog of ignorance—driven by the twin fates of biology and cosmology. Carretto suggests that to have discovered is to find oneself "at the doorway of eternity." To step into that doorway is the movement of life on earth.

Now we become *conscious of* not only of who we are as spiritual creatures, but conscious of the mystery of God who is the unique reality surrounding us. Now, the real learning can take place. To be conscious of God is to begin to pray—itself a self-transcending act. We can enter into communication with this divine mystery who is our creator as well as sustainer. We know that "in God we live and move and have our being." (Acts 17:28) To be conscious of God enables us to see fate as an illusion and providence as the mysterious gravity keeping us in the divine environment we call "our world."

Following Carretto's scheme, our life on earth can now *penetrate* and *contemplate* this mystery of God. These third and fourth steps go together. Having become conscious of God's presence, we penetrate it—we enter into it. We can actually "get into it." To penetrate God's presence is an involvement of learning. To be "in it" means we can contemplate it. This penetration and contemplation takes place in our heart. In his book, *Contemplative Prayer*, Thomas Merton says our heart is "the psychological ground of one's personality, the inner sanctuary where self-awareness goes beyond analytical reflection and opens out into metaphysical and theological confrontation with the Abyss of the unknown yet present—one who is 'more intimate to us than we are to ourselves.'" To be with God in our heart is to come to the threshold of knowing that our place is in God's space.

To cross this threshold of knowing is to *accept* this mystery of God's presence as the truth of our life on earth—to know it as good, to see it as beautiful, and by love to be brought into the fullness of its unity. This knowing—which is an acceptance of myself in God's space—is faithfully living my journey into the infinity of eternity. In his book, *Yoga and the Jesus Prayer Tradition*, Thomas Matus says this kind of "faith, when it is authentic, takes me beyond security into a realm where peace may indeed be found, but only in an unmoored drifting into the vast sea of reality."

This is the kind of faith which brings the peace of *loving* this mystery of God, the unique reality surrounding us. At the heart of this mystery is God's Heart—that Heart which loves our heart. In this loving I no longer have to understand myself as a lonely meteorite hurtling through a cold, limitless space heading nowhere except to death. It is now possible to see myself and feel myself able to have a home—to come home to my own place in God's space. Finally, with the words of Sharon Parks we realize, "it is here that *creator spiritus* meets us, in the midst, in the present, now in this dangerous moment, inviting us to be home-makers..."

We are not out-of-control meteorites, but spiritual astronauts who are heading home. In fact, our journey is a home-making pilgrimage. What a trip!

Chapter 4
Pilgrimage

What Person Do I Want To Be

As Christmas lurks around the corner, many of us feel ambivalent. On the one hand, there is excitement—anticipated joy, hoped for relational fulfillments which come from the season which celebrates God's entry and human involvement in our world. On the other hand, there is a kind of muffled groan—born from the memory of the seasonal excitement which superficially covers a deeper boredom, a memory of anticipated joys which frequently materializes as sadness, and a memory of relational hopes which finally are experienced as loneliness, or worse, rejection.

And yet, it is important once again to tell the Christmas story. As Alan Jones says in his book, *Passion for Pilgrimage*, "the only thing to do is to go on telling the story in as many different ways as possible in the hope that some new variation may awaken another human being and set him or her on pilgrimage." Christmas is the beginning story of God's incarnational pilgrimage on earth. The Christmas season is, indeed, the incarnational season—the time when the "Word became flesh and dwelt among us." (Jn. 1:14) For us, to participate in Christmas is ourselves to become incarnational pilgrims—ourselves to become words of the Word.

To become incarnational pilgrims is to become persons of *action*. It is instructive to know that the Latin term for the "Word" is Verbum—our English term for "verb." To become an incarnational pilgrim who continues to live out God's Christmas story in the world is to become God's verb— to be a verb of the Verbum. Verbs are terms of action, of motion, of movement. To be God's verb is to be God's "agent" in the world—to ensure there is some divine excitement instead of ecclesiastical boredom, to represent joy in those places where melancholy abounds, to befriend the quietly lonely.

To become an incarnational pilgrim is to become a person of *expression.* A verb is not only an action word; it is an expressive word. As one recent *Sports Illustrated* article has it from a football coach who neither believes in winning at all costs nor weight training, "I don't care if you can benchpress the world...I want you to be the best person you can be." Jesus would say the same to his "verbal imitators." The Army is not the only place which wants you "to be all you can be." In fact, ultimately the Army is not able to assist you in being all you can be. Only God can grace us with this possibility and grace us as we actualize that "growth into sainthood."

Finally, an incarnational pilgrim is a person of *perfection.* That is perfection, not perfectionism! A person of perfection is a graceful verb—acting/expressing herself and himself in conformity with God's will. It is to be open to seeing again and again how God's Word becomes words (disciples) and watch those words be expressed in lives of action and ministry. Once more, as Alan Jones says, "it is...a rule of the inner life that what is inside must come out." If God's Word has come into us, God's verb will come out! To tell the Christmas story again this year is one more rehearsal of a larger story of how strangers become friends of Jesus, the Word. The good news is not limited to hearing the history about a baby born in a Palestinian crib. The good news really is a contemporary assurance that God—through Jesus—continues "Verbally" to move in our world and bring more "verbs" into being. If Christmas gets inside us—truly—it must come out!

More Valuable Than Rubies

The most outstanding and effective men and women in our Christian heritage have taught the same lesson which men and women in any spiritual tradition teach. That lesson can be stated quite simply: the spiritual journey is a walk from being *vulnerable* to becoming *valuable*. The spiritual journey which does not pass through the portals of vulnerability is likely a journey which has become idolatrous for having chosen a god of security. Or, it is a journey which has become idyllic—sweet and pleasing, but out of touch with the seamy and the painful. Furthermore, the journey which does not lead us to become spiritually valuable is a journey which is illicit because we will have walked a worthless life.

Who among us does not know what it means to be vulnerable? One does not have to be a Latin scholar to know that *vulnerabilis* means that we can be "hurt" or "wounded." One only has to be human for a few days—much less a few years—to know that experience teaches us we can be hurt. We learn to cope in different ways. We try to avoid situations and places where we will be hurt. Sometimes, we try first to hurt so that we can not be "had." We run, we hide, we fight, we give up, we die—so we will not be hurt.

Sometimes, we acquire power or money to buy safety or to threaten. Or, we may choose to stay weak or poor so no one will ask anything or care about us. And yet try as we may, in the long run we cannot avoid the fact that we might get hurt. And the irony is, unless we are willing to get hurt, we will never know about love or about life. The spiritual journey is an ironical invitation—an invitation to life and love. And those realities usually pass through the portals of vulnerability.

The good news is the spiritual journey will *inevitably* become valuable. This journey takes life in a worthy direction. For it is only "on the way" with God that we realize what we most hope for and what we most fear might not be true: *the truth is we are already loved!* The journey teaches us how to live out of this gift of God's love—that we do not have to earn our way, fight our way or give up on the way.

Through Jesus our way is a way into our vulnerability—but, at the same time, a way beyond our vulnerability. It is a way through the death of our idolatrous, idyllic, illicit "self" by means of a rebirth into lovers of God and livers in God's world. In his book, *The Inner Loneliness,* Sebastian Moore dares add a ninth beatitude, namely, "blessed are the dead, for they shall be raised up to renew the earth."

We are valuable because we are God's seed—planted in God's world to renew the earth's promise to be fruitful. We are harbingers of this divine promise by bringing grace to those bound and bringing justice to those oppressed. People will come to know us through friendship—just as we came to know Jesus as friend. We are valuable because we are God's eternal spring-time being introduced to a winter-world having lost its freshness and its vigor.

Pathway To Peace

"The soul in search of the Word." (*Anima quaerens Verbum*) These words from a sermon of the twelfth century Cistercian, Bernard of Clairvaux, summarize the human spiritual journey. Our journey through life is nothing more than a journey back home—back to the Word of God who conceived us and brought us into being. In the opening words of his *Confessions* Augustine says that God stimulates us to praise. Augustine continues his address to God, "because you have made us for yourself...our hearts are restless until they can find peace in you."

The spiritual journey is the discovery of a pathway to peace. We find peace in God because our spirit is looking for its home. Sharon Parks talks about the power of the metaphor of journey when she says, as humans, "we do harbor a conviction that we are made for more." This is the cause of restless hearts—the realization that we were not made for boredom nor busyness. We were made for more—made for God, as Augustine proclaimed. Again, Parks comments that "our desire to soar (and the experience itself—the ecstatic high) is readily fused with a conviction of aliveness, a confidence of spirit." Our desire to soar is naturally ours because we have—or better—are spirit *(anima)*.

Our spirit looks for God—and the peace which ensues from a meaningful relationship with that divine Lover. Even the term, *anima,* suggests the dynamics of this relationship. *Anima,* or "spirit," is a word of motion, of engagement, and of excitement. People who are in touch with their spirit are "animated." They are alive, they are confident; those are the people engaged and excited about being alive and seemingly giving to the world more than they receive. And yet, they have already learned the paradox of divine love—the more you give, the more you receive! So they spend liberally!

The subject of the spiritual journey is clear: I am the subject—my *anima,* my spirit. The action of the subject is also clear. My spirit is the animated search for the Word who is God's self-expression in the world. The Latin word for "search" (*quaero*) is an instructive term. It means not only to seek or search for, but it also means to get or obtain. Confidently, we are assured our spirit's search for God will always be profitable. We ask and shall be given. We knock and to us it will be opened. In English we realize that *quaero* means we are on a "quest." Our spiritual journey is a quest; it is an adventure. Another way of seeing life in this spiritual sense is as an *animated adventure.*

For so many people, the sad truth is their sense that the only adventure they can hope for is a trip to Disneyland. They fail to see that their trip to Disneyland may well be fun—but, as an animated adventure, ultimately it is an illusion and, hence, disappointing. Disneyland does not affect our daily reality. Our spirits are searching for something more than Mickey Mouse. And God does not quack!

Walt Disney made a fortune out of make-believe. God made us for the divine self and gave us a spirit fit for unbelievable fortune—life and life abundantly. But God made it an adventure. God wants us to "come to something" which is what *ad-venio* (adventure) means. The spiritual journey is a coming to God, a divine adventure!

We come to God by our search for the Word (*Verbum*). The Word is the creative aspect of the divinity—a divinity who brought us into being (Genesis) and redemptively brings us into new being by becoming human that we might once more know God (John). The Word became human and dwelt (and dwells!) among us. The animated adventure is nothing more than the human search for the divinity disclosed in our very midst—in every human heart. Christians quite correctly talk about the "inward Christ." The incarnation is not merely a historical fact; it is a present and living reality. In his book, *The Crucified Jesus Is No Stranger,* Sebastian Moore captures well this animated adventure. He observes "in the spiritual life, the only motivational and inertia-shifting insights, the only ones that touch us in our indolence and so make a permanent differences to our lives, are those that have come from ourselves alone, discoveries. Bon voyage therefore!" Moore points to that place where discovery of the Word happens—in our hearts. To find the Word (in Latin, Verbum) is to find the place of divine activity in us—and in the world. It is the place where we are formed into a "verbal" expression of discipleship.

Obviously, *verbum* gives us the English word, "verb." Through Jesus, the incarnation becomes God's Verbal self-expression in the world. As the inward Christ, it is God's Verbal self-expression in each of us. A verb is a word of action. God's Word is the divine movement in a world seeking to go home. In Jesus we hear God saying, "Come to me: Follow me." As God's movement in the world, Jesus animates us for the quest—for the trip home.

This means the *journey* is not the final reality. The quest—life—is a trip home—which is the final reality. Our journey is home. We can get a glimpse of "home" when we realize this is part of the work of the church—to help people learn how to homestead. Sharon Parks says, "homemaking and homesteading are activities which build a space where souls can thrive and dream—secure, protected, related, nourished and whole."

If we could see the church as this kind of "home," going to church would not be so bad!

Get Out Of The Fast Lane

The age of the automobile has given our world and our language a number of interesting, descriptive phrases. To describe our busy lives, we coin a metaphor of the road. We are "living in the fast lane." Life lived in the fast lane has all the thrill of excitement and, often, as the popular sports show has it, "the agony of defeat." Frequently, the way we choose to live has a feeling of being fated. When it is no longer exciting or thrilling—or when the defeats unmercifully pile up—we cannot find our way off this life-style. Only a wreck ends it!

We dream of and yearn for a way of life which is authentic—one that is full of meaning and deeply satisfying. In the 1960's Thomas Merton published his book, *New Seeds of Contemplation.* He addressed the aborted longing we have for a life authentically lived in the Spirit. He allows, "it is the easiest thing in the world to possess this life and this joy; all you have to do is believe and love; and yet people waste their lives in appalling labor and difficulty and sacrifice to get things that make real life impossible."

Living life in the fast lane is to live with appalling labor and risk in order to get things which make real life impossible! The competitive drive to be rich or famous or successful often involves "passing others." Sometimes, it requires running others off their own roads—because in competition a winner demands a loser! In life, one can see these wrecks all over the place. Tragically, life lived in this fast lane is damaging and demeaning because *real* life has become impossible.

But—why do we find ourselves stuck in high gear, racing through meaningless jobs, not enjoying empty luxuries, numbly aware of life's corrosive qualities? "Sin," says Merton. Perceptibly, he notes, "we have to do violence to ourselves to keep from laboring uselessly for what is bitter and without joy..." Living in the fast lane is living in sin—in this case, sin is doing violence to oneself. The life-wrecks of our world are not simply crumpled bodies in damaged automobiles. The life-wrecks of our world are those of us "sinning" against our own real life possibilities—doing violence to our chances for joy and our hopes for love.

As long as we are careening along in our fast lanes, we are alone or together—but in competition. We are in bondage, committed to win rather than love. Within our world, the good news proclaims there always rests an alternative. *God is love*—and Jesus is God lovingly present in the world—bringing our madness to a halt and bringing joy in madness's place. Too often, however, we cling to our mad way of life and either ignore God or try to "take God for a ride."

But God is no fool, precisely because God is love. Eventually, God knows our ride finishes and our road dead-ends. And there God always lovingly will be—ready to take us home...safe and secure. God is a healer. In his book, *Simply Sane,* Gerald May assures us: we can understand something about God, because "treating your self with gentleness, accepting fully, seeing clearly, being fully as you are, being as neurotic as you are, healing might happen. Healing occurs when awareness is open and when acceptance is total." This is what coming home will give you. Come home. Be healed! Be whole! Be saved! They are all one!!

Kingdom Travel

A French Roman Catholic psychiatrist, involved in the spiritual formation of Catholic priests, has written a testy book challenging much of what passes for Christianity today. Pierre Solignac is particularly hard on the kind of Roman Catholicism he finds in his native France. He characterizes the church as "rigid and anxious...trying to survive in outmoded structures." He continues in his book, *The Christian Neurosis*, to say that "the church, like all neurotics, is bad at communicating with itself and the world around. Incapable of being creative, the institution, anxious and tense, is always on the defensive."

There would be little worry on the American part, and less reason to read Solignac, if he were describing a problem limited to French Catholicism. But, the institution he describes seems somehow to remind us of aspects of the American Christian experience—not seventeenth century Puritanism which in some ways was adventuresome, competent and creative. In too many ways, it describes modern Christianity. Solignac further comments that the church "obsessed with its personal problems...is turning in on itself. The church reminds one of those travellers who are always late, who have never stopped getting ready, jump on the train as it's going—and then discover they've caught the wrong one."

Actually, there really is only *one* Christian train. That is the train heading towards the kingdom—a kingdom of light and love, as early Christians might have put it. The kingdom-train is headed for a self-defined goal—but, if we become solely goal-oriented, we have lost the importance of the process of "getting there." Amazingly, to be on the kingdom-train evokes the feeling that the kingdom has, in part, *already* come. We kingdom travellers are going the right way, but getting there is fun as well!

Sadly, it is easy to reflect on oneself and one's fellow travellers and hear a great deal of grumpiness and, indeed, see too much grimness. It causes us to wonder if, in our lateness and ill-preparedness/selfishness, we have not breathlessly jumped on a train going the wrong direction and only are now discovering our misdirection. And some of us even are engineers!

Our misdirection is measurable by the grumpy fellow-travellers. Webster tells us to "grumble" is to make low, unintelligible sounds in the throat. Ironically, Jesus invites us to praise—and, instead, one hears unintelligible sounds in the throat! To grumble is to mutter or mumble in discontent. The mutterings and mumblings are throaty expressions of unhappiness with the process of being delivered to a new place. We are scared—unable to trust God and the liberating process of the kingdom-train. In the face of our fear we opt for the familiar—we choose bondage and exercise our preference for Egypt to the kingdom.

The mumbling and grumpy ones on the kingdom-train complain—complain in surly and peevish ways. To grumble is to be "rooted" in the grim, trapped in negativity. As Solignac says, "many people are discontent with themselves and, perpetually unhappy, let off steam on those around them. Overwhelming them and criticizing everyone and everything, they promenade their peevishness and their aggressive judgment in search of a new foolish victim on whom they can pour scorn." Welcome aboard the hellish-train!

This is not the time for a new year's resolution; something more real and radical is needed: a *spiritual transformation.* "The kingdom is at hand," Jesus proclaimed. (Mk. 1:15) Repent of your grimness and discover the joy of living. Repent your grouchy temper and learn to play—you are a child of God. Go find yourself a spiritual sandbox and begin to learn the play of the divine Spirit. Enjoy the frivolity of spiritual childhood. The bridegroom is with us! There is a divine party going on—don't be a party-pooper!

From Lent To The Cross

Ash Wednesdays come and go. They inaugurate the Christian season of Lent. For most Christians, Lent has lost its importance; indeed, most of us do not know that we are missing anything! Lent leads up to Easter and that is what carries importance for most Christians.

As I try to do each year, I attend an Ash Wednesday service somewhere besides my own place. For me, it is important once again to hear the Biblical truth about myself and every other creature of God. In the words from those services I am reminded that at our death, we will return to the earth. "You are dust and to dust you shall return." (Gen. 3:19) In the Christian context, the mortality of humankind is connected inextricably with the redeeming work of Jesus Christ. This connection is focused on the cross. The solemn point of the Ash Wednesday service is when there is made on our foreheads the figure of the cross.

Now the real, contemporary Christian fun begins! For me, the question is posed: do I leave the service by way of the bathroom and wash the ashes off my forehead? That way, I can resume my "normal" way of being in the world. Or, do I go into the secular world with what appears to be a bruise or a dirty head? People stare and do not know whether to ask, "what is wrong?" or pretend they do not see what I know they are staring at!

I have this year chosen to walk around in my world with the form of a cross made in ashes on my forehead. As a Christian, I know there is nothing special about that in itself. However, I also know it forces my reflection through self-examination. I realize how easy—as a Christian—it is to live *incognito* (unknown) in the world. I can look normal in every respect: clean, good clothes, etc.

This makes me examine whether and how I can be God's *symbol* in the secular world? Wearing jewelry in the form of a cross is a fairly safe and acceptable way to go. But, the real Christian question is how my "Ash Wednesday" will be symbolized on Thursdays or in September? Simply wearing jewelry cannot be my sole answer.

For me, Lent has not been a question of what I give up, but what I am willing to *take on*. I want to take on the joy of being Christ's disciple in the secular world. I want that joy to be visible and, in a sense, *sacramental*. Jesus did not call us every day to wear ashes on our foreheads. He did call us to be witnesses and friends to each other.

The real disciples are those who realize our call is not once a year to go into the world with crosses made of ash on our forehead. Rather, our call is to go into the world "and make disciples of all nations, baptizing them in the name of the Father and of the Son and of the Holy Spirit, teaching them to observe all that I have commanded you." (Mt. 28:19-20) In this we will be living witnesses to the power of Ash Wednesday—the cross and the resurrection.

Go Through The Work

In 1656 while in prison at Launceston, England, George Fox, the founder of Quakerism, wrote a powerful exhortation to Friends in the ministry. This letter contains the well-known phrase, "walk cheerfully over the world, answering that of God in every one." As so often is the case, we hear this cited and it inspires an optimism which aptly characterizes early Quakerism. But, this optimism can be naive if it is grounded in a superficial humanism. For me, it is only when I take seriously the context of walking cheerfully that I am able to imagine *actually* walking cheerfully.

Fox's letter, first of all, must be understood as directed to the *ministers* among Friends. Obviously, Quakers rightfully believe that all are called into discipleship and, consequently, called into ministry as well. But disciples are not immediately mature! Many disciples take some time discovering and growing into their ministries. But ministry is our call—a call to which we will learn "to answer that of God in every one." In his letter Fox tells us how this happens. We are to be "obedient to the Lord God and go through the work to be valiant for the Truth upon earth."

The phrase here which seems appropriate is to "go through the work." Becoming aware of and practicing one's ministry is a "work." It is a work— founded and grounded in the grace of God's sustaining call, but a work nevertheless. This work is captured poignantly in Fox's letter. He uses the agricultural metaphor of ploughing. "Plough up the fallow ground...And none are ploughed up but he who comes to the principle of God in him which he hath transgressed." Fox pursues the image when he allows that once we have ploughed (come to God's principle in us), "the planting and the watering and the increase from God cometh."

This tells us that learning to be a minister—and learning to "answer that of God in every one"—takes a season. Our ministry begins with the warming of a springtime. We plough by turning over the crust of our outer selves and digging down into those selves to find a heart. The heart is where we will find this principle of God. Everybody has a heart; it is this which we will "answer" in our ministries. As ministers, we are "living" in our hearts and looking to help others find and live in their hearts.

It is when we have "found" our heart—this principle of God—that we can understand why Fox says, "*then* you will come to walk cheerfully..." We will not need a bumper sticker to proclaim, "I found it." We will be living *lives of proclamation.*

As finders, we could be keepers! But having God's cheer, we want to give it away. We want to invite the world to God's party; *we* are the invitation. It will say something like "come to me, all you who labor and are heavy laden, and I will give you rest." (Mt. 11:28) The party is a ceasing from the worries of the world. Cheers!

Run The Good Race

Recently a friend of mine gave me a poster with a runner heading down a long hill only to have the long, up–hill run loom ahead. The poster looks as if one can see for two or three miles into the runner's future! The caption on the poster reads "the race is not always to the swift, but to those who keep on running." I very much appreciate the sentiments of this line. At my age and without the physical prowess of the younger runners, being swift is more memory than reality! Seriously, running has come to mean a number of things to me.

Perhaps, the most important issue which can be addressed is that one comes to understand that the "race" is the *running itself*—not the victory. While I cannot claim that running has brought me spiritual highs, it has been a formative and instructive exercise which analogously helps me understand the spiritual journey which brings us to our own finish lines.

The apostle Paul employs the image of running to describe the Christian journey. In his initial letter to Corinth Paul says, "Do you not know that in a race all the runners compete, but only one receives the prize? So run that you may obtain it. Every athlete exercises self–control in all things. They do it to receive a perishable wreath, but we an imperishable." (I Cor. 9:24–5)

Here Paul potentially misleads us if we understand that the Christian journey is like a race—and that only one person will "win" the race. All the rest of us would be like the "fun–runners" in a marathon. Surely, Paul is not expecting that there be one winner in the Christian race and the rest merely Christian fun–runners.

I can assure you that anyone who has completed a marathon is not simply a fun–runner—so, no Christian is Christian "just for fun." Rather, we have to see Paul suggesting that each of us finds his or her own Christian journey to be our own race—and that we each in our own way can "win." If each of us can win our own race—understood as our own journey—then the only way to lose is not to run. It is in this context one has to read what, for Paul, grammatically is an imperative: "So run!"

We can win *only* by running. As a runner, I know how important it is to train for running. The Christian journey has its comparable "training"—and we call these disciplines. The disciplines are many and varied, but include things like prayer, worship, and study. Not to be disciplined will injure both the runner and the Christian. For the runner, discipline builds endurance. One needs regularity in the exercise.

Discipline also builds endurance in the Christian. It enables us to make our way through the desert. For the Christian runner, the desert is the place where we are tried and we develop discipline to be winners. In his book, *Soul Making*, Alan Jones describes the desert as a "place of silence, waiting, and temptation. It is also a place of revelation, conversion, and transformation. In the desert we wait, we weep, we learn to live."

It will be from the desert—from running—that we learn to live. Many of us will learn to live—not because we are swift—but because we keep on running. Although we may fear that the desert place will be a lonely place, we will discover others will run with us and teach us how; these will be friends. The title of a well-known book, *The Loneliness of the Long Distance Runner*, can mislead us. Our "long distance" is life itself—and it does not have to be lonely. In fact, we will learn that actually we run—live—in a pack, "a core group" as Sebastian Moore calls it in his book, *The Inner Loneliness*. He writes, "Jesus formed a core group of disciples, men and women whom he invited into a closer relationship. These people picked up what a contemporary theologian has called the 'contagion' of Jesus." So, running—life—is contagious. Let's go!

Pilgrim People

"The true meaning of faith can be learned only on pilgrimage, and to the end of time the people of God will be the pilgrim people. But this is not an unaccompanied journey." These words by Stephen Neill in his book, *Jesus Through Many Eyes*, point to two truths of human life. The first truth is that the meaning of faith—indeed, life—is that of pilgrimage. Pilgrimage is being on the move. We move from conception to disintegration, from womb to tomb. Life has a myriad of possibilities, but there is no choice against pilgrimage. Once born, we must die; the only real question is whether the pilgrimage has meaning or will be given meaning. This is the potential "learning" of the pilgrimage.

This leads to the second truth of life, namely, that the pilgrimage need not be unaccompanied. Indeed, during the Easter season we who know the powerful re-creating presence of God through the resurrected Jesus know the full force of his parting words in Matthew's gospel: "and lo, I am with you always, to the close of the age." (Mt. 28:20) The reassurance of God's presence is a comfort to a people who are destined—even *as* God's people—to be a pilgrim people to the end of time.

Being Christian is not license to drop out of life or to quit the journey. Rather, to be Christian is to join the pilgrim people who are learning about life *with* meaning—movement *with* purpose—love *with* fulfillment. The Christian paradox is that life, movement and love so often find their meaning, purpose and fulfillment in ironical ways. Because of this irony, the journey of the Christian always goes directly through the cross. Suffering and giving over are frequently the hallmarks of this Christian irony. In this sense, Christians in the world are always a *pathetic* pilgrim people.

Even the word, "pathetic," carries this irony. On the street the normal usage of the term, "pathetic," means sorry or pitiful or weak. In that sense, no one would want to be a pathetic person. However, the Greek root meaning of the word pathetic is *pathos*. *Pathos* keys us directly to the suffering which Jesus experienced on the cross. *Pathos* is the opposite of apathy. As the embodiment of God's love lived out with purpose and giving meaning to life, Jesus was a pathetic figure.

In his weakness he ironically demonstrated, ultimately and unconditionally, the strength and power of God's love. In his pitiful lack of respect and demeaning treatment by the powerful, he transformed our understanding of power and authority as they give meaning to life. Finally, from his sorry impotence on the cross, he pronounced the loving word of forgiveness on the world, "Father, forgive them, for they know not what they do." (Lk. 23:34)

Jesus—the pathetic figure—invites all of us to journey with him. To become a pilgrim people is to become "pathetic"—pathetic in a caring, loving way. How ironical to realize that only pathetic people know life as meaningful, purposeful and fulfilled! Concretely, we know this in a group—as pilgrim people. Practically, we know it through friendship. Jesus knew what he was doing when he called us "friends." Rise up, O people of God, we are going on a pilgrimage!

Visit A Friend

Tucked away in a little courtyard in what is now an apartment complex in York, England, are a number of Quaker graves. Among them is the famous American Quaker and anti-slavery leader, John Woolman. Visitors to York usually do not know about Woolman. Quaker visitors to York normally are not aware Woolman died there from smallpox in 1772. Fewer even contemplate a visit to the Bishophill graveyard to remember the one whom the contemporary Quaker, Elton Trueblood, calls "the most authentic saint who has emerged in the Quaker movement."

At the entrance to the private apartment complex which contains Woolman's grave is this simple sign: "In the gardens of this house, a former Quaker burial ground, are the graves of many Friends, including JOHN WOOLMAN, WILLIAM ALEXANDER, WILLIAM and ESTHER TUKE and LINDLEY MURRAY. Friends who wish may visit them."

What a lovely invitation—Friends who *wish* may visit them. "Come on in," we are beckoned. Opening the gate, one proceeds into the courtyard to observe lovely flowers, green grass and around the wall there are small, uniform gravestones. Approaching one simple gravestone, visitors can read, "Near this stone rest the remains of John Woolman..."

We step back—maybe a little disappointed. A great Quaker saint with such a remarkable life and an *unremarkable* grave in an out-of-the-way location in one of England's most stunning cities. No wonder hardly anyone bothers to visit the graves here in this former Quaker burial ground...now housing living people! "So what," the world could utter, its citizens more interested in a York known in Roman times as *Eboracum* and from where in 306 A.D. Constantine was declared emperor of the Roman empire. "Who cares about a little, obscure Quaker grave," the world complains, "when there is a magnificent York cathedral to visit!"

Ah, but the truth is to perceive what that burial ground sign could really mean when it says of Woolman and others, "Friends who wish may visit them." Contemporary Christians can visit Woolman better by going to his *Journal* than by going to York. In a world where MTV assaults our senses—or soap operas seductively numb our feelings—Woolman is still here in spirit and truth. His grave is in York and his book is on the shelf. You do not need a plane ticket; rather, his *Journal* is the ticket to plain truth.

The key is to realize the move is up to us. The saints of our world are those who have visited God—or better, have welcomed God's visitations in their lives. A saint has not only been hospitable to God, the visitor, but made a home in his or her heart for God's Spirit to dwell. Jesus is still God's visitor in our world—as he was for Woolman's world. Jesus says, "Behold, I stand at the door and knock; if any one hears my voice and opens the door, I will come in to him and eat with him, and he with me." (Rev. 3:20)

If we open our hearts, Jesus comes as guest—and, if we wish, he becomes a friend. At some point in simple, ordinary, maybe out-of-the-way places, he appears and knocks. We hear his voice and it speaks truth. He nurtures us into an abundance of life. To invite Jesus to set up his abode in our heart is to give up all self-seeking. In the words of Joann Wolski Conn in her book, *Spirituality and Personal Maturity*, we are "then free to seek God on whom I am dependent and who is present at the heart of my true self."

Chapter 5
Motions and Moods

Be A Friend

Most of us arise in the morning and find our way to the bathroom to begin making ourselves attractive to the world. Some try to grow hair, others cut it. We spend time looking "natural." For some, age has a way of eroding the possibility of looking "good," while for others, age adds grey—making them look distinguished and wise. Interesting it is that grey hair is linked with grey matter! Pondering this does not lure me to suggest that we avoid the bathroom in a return to the hippy scene, but it does expose the tip of an old spiritual iceberg, namely, the issue of *vanity*.

We can begin to think about vanity by considering its synonym, pride. As we know, pride is a "spiritual no–no." Pride smacks of having things disordered: God in second place—or no place—and the self in first place—or the only place. Vanity is a subtle or sophisticated pride. We get a handle on it when we look at its root meaning.

In Latin, it is *vanus* or *vanitas*. It is translated with words such as emptiness, uselessness, and boastful. "To run in vain" is to run with no hope of succeeding to one's goal. Spiritually speaking, we run in vain when we put our "self" in such a place of importance that it can never bear the weight of reality. Concretely, this happens when we place too much emphasis on how we look, what kind of car we drive, how smart we are or who our actual or imagined forbearers were. These are what might be called "positive vanities" in the sense that they are things we have or are which (vainly) make us feel important, advantaged or good.

There are also what might be called "negative vanities" which often serve to excuse people from living in right relationship with God. Such vanities are being unattractive, too old or young, dumb, unlucky and so on. Certainly these are seen as causes for discrimination by a world which often rewards the "positive vanities." But sadly, those who define their "self" with negative vanities have not yet heard the good news from God. Negative vanities are just as delusive as the positive; the fact remains: vanity is delusive and valueless in any of its forms.

In the final analysis, vanity does not have to do with how you look, how much money you make or brains. Vanity has to do with our "self." When our true self is not seen in the context of the creator God, then we are tempted to make ourselves "gods." This is vain, empty and futile. When we choose to live to ourselves and not to God, then we have winked at reality—and live vainly.

In this place we need most friends who will not confirm our vanity, but rather friends who help us understand reality. Our friends become the "bathroom of reality," doing for our true self what the mirror does for our vanity. Our friends reflect to us what really matters, call and encourage us to live in that divine reality and celebrate with us the authenticity of the life of the spirit.

In her book, *Faithful Friend*, Dorothy C. Devers details what this process looks like in the relationship of two people. She says "in this endeavor we are being present to, praying for and with our friend...Thus does one strengthen the other, help him to grow spiritually...and in turn is comforted, confronted, and strengthened by the other."

So, don't be vain—be a friend!

Pleasing To God

The only thing worse than looking at someone's vacation pictures is having to be present when their children are "showing off!" Everyone of us has been subjected to the antics of some show–off. Most of the time we endure it—sometimes even with a smile and a sarcastic snip, "that's nice!" The real problem, however, is when the "show-of" comes into his or her adult years. Showing off is still an attempt to gain attention.

Typically, a show–off is not "showing" anything except a need to be needed. This need is even more pronounced in adults. Sadly, Christian women and men are not immune from this showing off phenomenon. Among adults, it takes many forms. Sometimes it is the playful, foolish actions; sometimes it is the gossiping, slandering, back–biting approach to one's friends and neighbors. Typically, our approach is to make someone look bad or foolish and thereby we "apparently" get attention.

As adults, we can usually identify this as an attempt to be *pleasing*. Too often, we think that if we can only please the other person, he or she will like us. As humans, our need to be needed usually takes the form of trying to make someone dependent upon us. Upon closer examination, however, our attempt to be pleasing usually makes us the dependent ones! We try to project an image or develop a reputation which we think will "attract" the others, making them like and accept us.

If they accept us, we then feel the necessity to continue projecting that image in fear that the other will not like us if we turn out to be different than they think we are. Hence, we become slaves to an image of our self we think the other will like. To be pleasing usually means to be in bondage—bound to a half–truth or, worse, to a false self. We are driven to the place where we can not afford to risk being our true self because the other may not be pleased.

When we think about what God wants from us, we realize that God does not want us to be or act from this potentially inauthentic place. God has met us *where* we really are and knows *who* we really are. What is bad can be forgiven; what is good is acknowledged and developed. God calls us not to be pleasing but to be *obedient*. For many of us, the dilemma is that God's call to obedience may, in fact, make us unpleasing to the other.

True Christian disciples turn out to be radicals. They are radicals, not because they have long hair, but because they take the gospel seriously. Their goal is not to be liked by everyone but to be *witnesses*—to show God, not to show-off. Mother Teresa is not a show-off; she is a powerful witness for the radicality of Christian obedience. When Jesus told Pilate that his kingdom was not of this world, he was declaring something profound about his appeal. The gospel proclamation is designed to speak truth and power to the human, sinful condition, not one to please the status quo.

Jesus showed us that the only way to be pleasing to God is to be obedient. When you know this, you will not only find that God likes you— but you will discover God truly *loves* you. Indeed, God loved us into relationship—into friendship. When we are loved this way, we do not have to please anybody. Instead, we will turn out to be pleasing—living lives fragrantly and beautifully. We will become the divine scent in a culture of polluted smells.

The Need For Balance

On a recent trip I had the opportunity to fly in a very small commuter plane. As the pilot climbed into her place, she took one look and asked me and another passenger if we would move to the rear so the plane would be balanced! My first thought was to be aware of how nervous I had become! Then, I decided the pilot probably knew what she was talking about—so I moved. Then, I began to ponder what it means to be balanced.

As a word, "balance" goes back to the Latin, *libra,* which means scales or level. From the Latin word, *equilibrium,* we get our English word, "equilibrium." All of us know the scales which are used to weigh something. One puts the object in one dish and adds corresponding weights in another dish until equilibrium is reached; then, you can know how much the object weighs. "To hang in the balance" is a phrase we use as we envision the slightly swaying scales registering the proximity of equilibrium. All of this flashed through my mind as I climbed to the rear of the plane to bring equilibrium!

Perhaps most of us were initially introduced to "balance" in our early school years on the playground teeter-totter. Quickly, we realized that we had to be paired with one nearly our own size or we would never balance. Up and down, up and down—we rhythmically would move. It was almost effortless. There was an ease when we were balanced. I like to use this as an image for the spiritual journey. The spiritual journey also can go as effortlessly and easily when there is balance.

Spiritually, we also have to become properly weighted if the movement picks up and lets us down. The too serious (grave) person is as if already dead. You—or even God—cannot move that person with ease! A Christian with no levity or sense of humor or easiness is not one with whom anyone wants to play. On the other hand, a spiritual lightweight is too easily lifted. He or she is no fun because they are always needing protection. You can never say anything slightly provoking or look the wrong way or—boom! The imbalance makes the teeter-totter crash—with hurt all around.

If we push the image further, we realize that Jesus is the friend who shows up in our life's playground and invites us to play. He climbs on the teeter-totter and the weight is always perfect. He matches everybody's weight and with a wink always says, "let's play." When we learn how, he climbs off and lets another one of his friends climb on. Then, we realize another follower of his has just taken his place.

In fact, the world's playground is where we, as his followers, are looking for other friends with whom we can play the spiritual game. Truly to learn about play is to learn something about the nature of love. In his book, *The Christian at Play*, Robert K. Johnston says "there is a spontaneity and an abandon which characterizes...play. Any lover knows this." The spiritual person proclaims, "it is playtime...let's go to the playground...and be with God!"

To Give What Is Yours

The history of the Christian church is full of instructive devotional literature which aids us on our pilgrimage in the faith. One of my favorite resources is a collection of stories from the fourth and fifth centuries called, "The Sayings of the Fathers." These are usually short, pithy stories which come from monks who were living in the Egyptian desert. They were men and women who had withdrawn from the routine of the secular life around them and, indeed, from the "business as usual" of the Christians in the world.

One of my favorite stories is about two old monks who had become so spiritual that they found it impossible to fight. The story goes that "two old men had lived together for many years without a quarrel. One said to the other: 'Let us have one quarrel with each other, as is the way of men.' And the other answered: 'I do not know how a quarrel happens.' And the first said: 'Look, I put a tile between us, and I say, That's mine. Then you say, No, it's mine.' And he answered: 'Yes, it is yours. Take it away.' And they went away unable to argue with each other."

For me, this is a wonderfully challenging story because I still know how to quarrel! In this way, I know that I still know "the way of men" which is nothing more than the way of the world—the way of being outside of God's presence. I know very well what is "mine." Knowing what is mine can put me in touch with that potential for selfishness which lay at the very heart of the ability to fight. Selfishness and possessiveness go hand in hand. I want to protect "mine."

There is still too much of the two-year old in all of us who are chronologically adults. It is as if we are in our own sandbox—called the world. In our particular section of the box called the United States, we are the loudest in yelling "mine!" Moreover, we are first to throw sand to keep the others away from mine. To read the story of the two monks places us back in the challenge of the love-message of Jesus, our Lord.

What would it mean to say to a world in need—when that world looks at "mine" and asks for something—to say, "Yes, go ahead and take it; it is now yours. Take it away." That would mean we are no longer selfish, that we are now true disciples of the one who admonished us to follow him. We would truly become friends of Jesus and friends to the world.

Grace Abounds

Aelred of Rievaulx, a twelfth century Cistercian monk, said it best in his treastise, *Spiritual Friendship*. "And so in friendship are joined honor and charm, truth and joy, sweetness and good-will, affection and action. And all these take their beginning from Christ, advance through Christ, and are perfected in Christ." To be perfected in Christ is to know the peace which passes all understanding and which takes away the causes of conflict.

Recently in Quaker meeting for worship a friend spoke out of the silence. This in itself is not striking. As usual, what was striking was both the content of the message and the passion with which it was shared. Actually, the words were simple; it was the impact of those words which was frightening in their truth and compelling in their challenge again to engage God and God's people. The simplicity of the words were that we were frequently "clumsy" in our interactions with our neighbors. I was caught by that image, a clumsy person.

The synonyms for clumsy I do not like: they suggest awkwardness, ineptitude, unwieldy, unskilled—even graceless. Intrigued by the word, clumsy, I pursued it back to its probable Middle English roots to discover that it conveyed the sense of being "numbed by the cold." Following out this thought, I realized that even a skilled person could become clumsy if numbed by the cold. An agile person could become awkward if numbed. Something which once worked smoothly can, in the face of numbing coldness, become unwieldy. The key to clumsiness is not badness but *numbness.* Often we are clumsy in our relationships with people, not because we are bad, but because we have been numbed by the cold and, therefore, have become awkward.

Spiritually speaking, where does all this lead? I have been aware for a long period of time that one of the ways God's Spirit is experienced by people is with a "warming" or even "hot" sensation. With God in their lives, people actually "feel" warmer. Indeed, some people have literally or figuratively "felt on fire" for God. What we begin to realize is that the Spirit of God can work on our numbness—melting our coldness, thereby making us less clumsy in relationship.

If we are warmed by the divine Spirit, we will relax and become aware of the "me" God truly wants us to become. We will realize that the "real me" is relationally able and aptly fitted to be present to and for the other. We will know this is true because we already know the truth of it with God who is the Absolute Other. What we discover is that the "real me" always requires a "real thee!"

The disciples discovered their "real me" when they encountered Jesus. They did not discover the truth of who they were by navel-gazing, but encountered in Jesus a "thee" who surely and powerfully led them simultaneously to God and to their "real me." In this encounter, Jesus was not clumsy but "grace-ful." He was graceful because he gave himself—which was the gift of God. What he received, in turn, was the relationship of friends. As friends, we too are called to be grace-ful with our neighbors.

It is only when we have ourselves set in relationship—and "I" for a "Thou"—that we can experience and savor the love which the gospel is all about. In the classic book, *I and Thou*, Martin Buber captures this when he says "love is between *I* and *Thou*... The man who does not know this, with his very being know this, does not know love...Love is responsibility of an *I* for a *Thou*..."

Where this kind of love abounds, there is no possibility for clumsiness—for grace abounds!

Kingdom Living—Now

For good reasons the Easter-Pentecost season always brings to mind the opening words of ministry which Jesus proclaims. Early in Mark's gospel we are told "Jesus came into Galilee, preaching the gospel of God, and saying, 'The time is fulfilled, and the kingdom of God is at hand; repent, and believe in the gospel.'" (Mk. 1:14-15) The nearness of the kingdom of God which Jesus proclaimed and into which he lived seemed, at first, blunted and even denied by his crucifixion. Then, comes the message of Easter announcing that "He Lives!" For Christians to understand that Jesus lives is to hold fast to the reality and nearness of that kingdom.

The nearness of the kingdom has sometimes been seen as contingent upon Christ's second coming. This position argues that until the Lord returns, the kingdom is not present or real. This, it seems, misunderstands the condition of the kingdom which Jesus himself proclaimed. He indicated that the kingdom is already at hand for those who repent and believe in the good news of God's involvement in history. So it is one's faith—one's trust in God—that is the condition for knowing the kingdom and its real presence.

From thinking about this and reading in monastic literature, I have seen what look like contradictory responses to the presence of God's kingdom received through faith. In the first response, any one of us who has come to know first-hand God's presence in our lives feels a compelling *urgency* to move more fully and more quickly towards God's person. We are urgent to fall more deeply in love with God, to explore more profoundly the intimacy with Jesus Christ. This urgency leaves us energized and eager to get on with our spiritual lives—to live into the fulness of the kingdom of God. We already know something about the joy, peace and love of God and are urgent for the fullness of the presence of God's kingdom. In this sense, a Christian ought to be in a hurry—knowing full well where she or he is going!

On the other hand, any one of us who has experienced the presence of God's hand on our lives is spared any anxiety or urgency about our destiny or the destiny of the world. We are brought to a place where, at times, we are told to wait. We will be brought to places of quietness and stillness where we are to go "no-where" and do "no-thing." As George Fox so frequently put it, we are to "wait upon the Lord." In this vein, waiting is not despair nor is it passivity. It is staying in that place of faith to which God always comes to meet and greet us.

Waiting will be *urgent* waiting. It will be eagerly waiting for more of God—more fully, more deeply God's kingdom and our own involvement in it. In tandem with waiting, urgency keeps us zealously focused and enthusiastically directed. When we have learned about this kingdom, then we too will go proclaiming its reality—urgently, but content to wait for God to do the divine work immediately in the heart of another.

Being in this kingdom takes away any need for the distress associated with life outside the kingdom. In his book, *Adam and Eve and Pinocchio*, physician, Willard Gaylin, writes "almost all psychic distress is the product of distorted perception that transforms our present reality, undervalues our strengths, and anticipates a dreaded imagined doom that tragically may arrive—precisely and only because it is anticipated."

Theologically, this means that outside of the kingdom we can have hell—have it anytime we want it through our psychic distress. Your choice: doom or the bridegroom!

Discipline—We All Need It

Recently I was rushing around an airport. That promoted some thoughts on impatience. I realized that I had "lost my patience." If I had lost it, I might have once had it!

Patientia is the Latin behind "patience." It means to endure, bear, suffer from or experience. When I have "lost" my patience, I know I have become short, curt, annoyed—maybe outright angry. I become restless and hurried. I also realized that I usually have one of two responses when I "loose it." One response is to strike out, take over or wait no longer. I move on—and move quickly! The other response is that I quit or walk away from whatever has caused me to lose my patience. My patience turns into a radical kind of passivity.

Patience always has been an important issue in spiritual growth and development. In this context one can be more and more aware of how Americans, at least, live in an age of "microwave theology." Like food, we expect faith to come packaged and prepared to be stuck in an ecclesiastical microwave and in thirty seconds be ready for spiritual consumption! We do not want to "waste time" in preparation of the experience of nurture.

This model of microwave theology can use the church as the supplier of the food. On one hand, the church can be like the fast-food chains. The church can be the provider of a kind of "Golden Arches faith" which can be stuck in its microwave. This is a church that will feed you fast—with no muss or fuss. The problem is you get only what they give. The experience in faith is always like the hamburger with the pickle, mustard—and only that way because we make nothing to suit who you are! You can not be *unique* or even special.

A different model of the microwave church is that church is a grocery store. Here you get the food—but still with little fuss. You have to stick it in the microwave, but nothing more. You can get the milk, but never see the cow. You can get the corn, but never hoe the rows.

What seems true about authentic spiritual growth is that it requires patience—patience because it takes time, requires endurance and experience. Patience is learned as a discipline. It is *discipline* which provides the church with a time-honored alternative to microwave theology. Discipline is the key to growth. Discipline enables us to develop our relationship with God and in relationship with the friends of God. In her book, *Metaphorical Theology*, Sallie McFague identifies some characteristics of that relationship: "mutuality, respect, acceptance of differences, cooperation, solidarity, attraction, perseverance, tolerance, gift-giving, delight, sacrifice, constructive criticism."

These characteristics can be developed as our relationship with God deepens and our friendship with God's people is cultivated. To know God is to be called into the art of making friends. It takes time to be patiently creative. Friendship is the patient, creative development of relationship. Spiritual friendships are those relationships which artfully develop with God at the center and with Christ as the cement of the bond and the Spirit as the energy of the growth.

No hurry—it all will be yours!

Stay In Truth

One significant problem which affects many of us in our relationships is ambivalence. Ambivalence leaves us feeling torn between two or more feelings or desires. We will find it is important to think about ambivalence in relationships because, at the heart of our involvement with God, we often discover the problem of ambivalence. We want to serve God—and we don't. We want to take time for God—but we don't.

We can better understand this problem of ambivalence with God when we understand how we are ambivalent in human relationships—even with those we most love. John Dunne, a contemporary theologian, suggests "that whenever we love a person, there is a good chance that we will also hate that person, because a person who can cause great joy in our life also can—and usually does—cause great pain." Commenting on Dunne's remarks, Walter Conn in his work, *Christian Conversion,* describes what many of us no doubt have often felt: "Thus, in a deep personal relationship there is often simultaneously hope and disappointment, confidence and fear, trust and mistrust, affection and resentment." And we realize all this with our friends! Who needs enemies?

But where does all this ambivalence take us—as if we do not know? Again, Conn is helpful when he declares that "so powerful is the desire for an unambivalent relationship of pure, unadulterated love, that we are tempted to end a relationship rather than live with its intolerable uncertainty." Indeed, it is all too well known how we and others have "quit" friendships for this very reason. We have given many "reasons," but the intolerable uncertainty explains much for us. For many of us, there are additional steps we tried before we "quit."

Often, we tried to ignore the other. We threatened or tried to control our friends. In all this, what we were trying to gain is certitude in our relationship. But, Dunne is clear when he acknowledges with this quest for certainty in relationships comes "the self-defeating quality that the pursuit of certainty always seems to have: the more desperately one seeks for certainty the more intensely one is plagued by uncertainty."

This is precisely the place where God enters our relational picture. Because the very nature of my relationship with God is faith, the possibility for ambivalence exists even with God! To know this, means I cannot seek certainty with God any more than with my friend. In faith and by trust, I can come to be secure with God and I can be confident with God—but I can never be certain. I can be certain what I feel or think, but I cannot be certain—for God, like a friend, is "other" than myself.

That is why God became human, to befriend us and teach us about relationships which are healthy, constructive and, ultimately, meaningful. When Jesus comes, he offers this relationship in friendship. Richard Bach in his allegorical story, *Jonathan Livingston Seagull,* tells how Jonathan finally comes back to the flock from which he had been cast out. Most of us are like those gulls of the flock who have not been befriended. We need Jonathan!

Like Jesus, "the more Jonathan practiced his kindness lessons, and the more he worked to know the nature of love, the more he wanted to go back to Earth. For in spite of his lonely past, Jonathan Seagull was born to be an instructor, and his way of demonstrating love was to give something of the truth that he had seen to a gull who asked only a chance to see truth for himself."

When we finally see truth for ourselves, we will not be ambivalent anymore. When we are ambivalent with God, we have stepped out of the truth. Stay in truth—and go with the flock of confident believers!

CHAPTER 6
THE HEART of LOVE

Practice The Presence

"The world is filled with a host of sad people." This passing comment from a friend grabbed me and began gnawing on my mind. Surely, all of us have known a sad moment and, doubtlessly, have endured longer periods of sadness which come close to the accompanying feeling of depression. The dictionary notes that depression is an emotional "sunkenness" which is greater and lasts longer than reality would suggest is appropriate. Depression is an emotional term, a psychological state of being.

In addition to being a psychological state, we could also suggest that depression is experienced as an issue of spirituality—and is better known there as melancholy. Melancholy is a feeling of sadness or depression because God does not seem either to be in the picture or, if in the picture, God is not helpfully or supportively or joyfully there.

The often-given advice to a sad person to "cheer up" and the exhortation to the depressed person to "shape up" sorely misses the mark. To "miss the mark" is one definition of sin; hence, to offer this easy advice in the face of depression and melancholy is tantamount to sinning. Rather, what we need and what we need to offer in those places of sadness—depression and melancholy—is a sense that we are not alone and that there is a future that is worth living. We can know that, in most cases of sadness and depression, there is some grief. With grief there always is a sense of loss or lack.

The problem with sadness, depression and melancholy—when they last too long—is that we no longer care. The problem becomes even more encompassing than not caring about the particular person or event which made you sad;

you come to care no longer about *anybody*—and that even includes yourself! In this sense, sadness/depression is unlike anger. People survive anger and other emotional upsets—but eventually sadness is a killer, because one ultimately experiences the death of loneliness.

Psalm 139 opens with these words: "O Lord, thou hast searched me and known me." (Ps. 139:1) When we spiritually know our innate relationship with God, we know there can be no ultimate sadness and no eternal basis for our depression. There is no basis for this because *ultimately* there is joy and *eternally* there is companionship. To know this is powerful and, yet for too many, either it is a not-knowing or it is a knowing filled with awe because it feels "awful"—potentially terrorizing. It means I cannot hide from God. It means I cannot deal in illusions with the One who knows. The temptation is to become atheistic or get depressed—simply because there is One who knows.

Actually, there is a third choice—a choice which is the *only* choice for life. I can engage the One who knows and realize, for this God, "knowing is loving." If God truly knows me, God actually loves me. The Old Testament is clear that truly to "know" somebody is to love her or him. For God, knowing is the language of intimacy rather than intimidation. God is love because God knows us.

This divine knowing is the eternal antidote for depression and melancholy. We are known and loved. We are not alone—hence, we need not be lonely. In turn, we will be able to love others insofar as we know them. To the sad, then, we will learn not to say, "cheer up," but come, let me know you. To the depressed, we will not say, "shape up," but come, let me love you. The beautiful, spiritual reciprocity is to realize at different times all of us will be both giver and receiver.

In this, we come close to the advice of Brother Lawrence who says the "secret is just this: (the faithful) responds completely to inward promptings either by elevating his heart to God, or by a quiet but genuine and fond regard of God, or by the words love forms."

Learning to do this means we will not be practicing depression or melancholy. We will be practicing the presence of God. Go forth in joy!

Jesus—Love—Friendships

Friendship is love. C.S. Lewis declares "when either Affection or Eros is one's theme, one finds a prepared audience...but very few modern people think Friendship a love of comparable value or even a love at all." It has taken me some time to realize that friendship is love. That awareness arises from careful attention to the biblical tradition.

The biblical passage which highlights friendship as love is John 15. Jesus tells his disciples that "this is my commandment, that you love one another as I have loved you. Greater love has no man than this, that a man lay down his life for his friends. You are my friends if you do what I command you. No longer do I call you servants, for the servant does not know what his master is doing; but I have called you friends..." (Jn. 15:12-15) In order to understand how friendship is love, one needs to know that the term, "friends," in this passage translates the Greek word, *philos*. It is appropriate to translate *philos* as "friend," but it is more important to realize this is one of three Greek words for "love." When we perceive that Jesus is talking about friendship *as love*, we come clearer as to what Jesus wants those disciples to comprehend.

In the gospel of John the disciples are given only one commandment by Jesus, to love one another. The model for this love is the love Jesus himself demonstrated to those same disciples. In effect, what Jesus commands is friendship! He befriended some rather unusual people and, consequently, they emerged as disciples. What these disciples (friends) realize—as the gospel unfolds—is both the *basis* of friendship and the *goal* of that friendship.

The basis of Jesus' friendship is God's love for God's creatures. The incarnation is the human expression—through

Jesus—of that divine love. The goal of the love of God—expressed through Jesus—is the establishment of a community of men and women who have learned from Jesus how to love one another. To be a friend of Jesus means to be a lover of other humans—who themselves are God's creatures and also objects of that same divine love.

It is well known that Quakers carry the name, "Friends," and have a special opportunity to be what their name suggests. To be a Friend (Quaker) is to be a lover—not in an erotic sense, but in a Christian sense. So, Quakers have a name to live up to. In fact, this is exactly what all Christians are called to live up to—to be lovers in God's world.

Simply to be called "friends" hides the real dynamite of the call of God—a call to be lovers of the divine and of each other. It is time to actualize the agape!

Learning And Loving

Charlotte Bronte's nineteenth century novel, *Jane Eyre*, is one of the more profound English works of literature. It is the story of a sad, but very strong, charity girl growing up in Victorian England. It deals with the age-old question: how do humans come to terms with life?

In the initial phase of Jane's life—her girlhood years at Gateshead—we see her living with a family where deprivation was her norm. She describes a Christmas season at the Reed household where her rich cousins, John, Eliza and Georgiana were participants in the festivities and gaieties. She was condemned to watch from the stairway. When she tired of watching, she would "retire from the stairhead to the solitary and silent nursery: there, though somewhat sad, I was not miserable." In a symbolically loaded passage Jane tells us that in the nursery she "sought shelter from cold and darkness in my crib."

We do not have to be charity-children to know a bit of this experience of sadness—of alienation and loneliness. Even those of us who are more like the cousins—invited to the parties of the world—know also the threat, if not the reality, of the cold and dark sides of life. We are threatened with being alone. We know what it is like to be sad; for many people, sadness eventually becomes misery.

As Jane goes to bed, she takes her doll. Through some powerful words she reflects "human beings must love something, and, in the dearth of worthier objects of affection, I contrived to find a pleasure in loving and cherishing a faded graven image, shabby as a miniature scarecrow." Somewhere in the cribs of our cold hearts we all have had—and many hold on presently—to our "dolls."

Human beings must love something. The fecundity of the spiritual world can take the place of our "dolls." Spirituality is an opening to any "boy or girl" in the world—an opening lives. Few of us would think ourselves able to live in God alone— because we have other plans, more pressing things to do.

We have wars to fight, jobs to do, television to watch, fun to have. We have egos to satisfy. Ego thrives on what we want—what we think we need. Ego predominates over heart and denies divine demands. And so, we can say with pride, "I poured my heart into that project." With just as much ego one can lament, "I lost heart." Someone has said suicide is a very egocentric act! Not to know our heart is to set ourselves up as god. We take charge—we take heart!

But, we are not god; we can never "take heart,"—we *have* a heart—God's gift to each of us. And that gift comes with a demand—to live in God alone. This is because, ultimately, it is only with our hearts that we can truly know what it means to live. And real life is in God and in God alone. To our hearts, God will come to be known as love. This is our call—really our heart's demand—to fall in love.

In his book, *The Road to Daybreak*, Henri Nouwen acknowledges, "I realized that God's love is a jealous love. God wants not just a part of me, but all of me. Only when I surrender myself completely to God's parental love can I expect to be free from endless distractions, ready to hear the voice of love, and able to recognize my own unique call." This is a contemporary way of reading Hadewijch's counsel.

Spiritually, the heart's demand, is always a road to Easter. It is both a way of death and way of life. As usual, Jesus shows us the Easter way and it is one we more readily read about than practice. As Nouwen says, the heart's demand is recognition that God wants "all of me." God does not want all those parts of me which are not really me: the egotistic achievements and failures of a lifetime's effort. God wants the real me, all of me. Actually, God demands it! In this demand is God's love. But that love is a way of death to our egotistical aspirations.

The real me—sustained by God's love—travels the Easter road to the cross. Nouwen says, "the way is the way of the cross, and true freedom is the freedom found in the victory over death." To follow the demand of our heart is to follow Jesus, the one who enjoins "I am the way, and the truth, and the life...(and) I came that they may have life, and have it abundantly." (Jn. 14:6, 10:10) Paradoxically, the "demand" of the heart turns out to be a gift! Surrender—which makes so many of us rebel—turns out to bring freedom. The way of death delivers us into abundant life.

Having come to abundant life returns us to the beginning: the demand of our heart is to live in that alone. And yet, as Nouwen poignantly allows, "the most radical challenge came out of the question, 'Is Jesus truly enough for you, or do you keep looking for others to give you your sense of worth?'" In this sense, the heart's demand is always "a struggle to let go of many idols along the way and to choose again and again to follow Jesus and him alone." With these words, it is easy to see why anything else will lead to a spiritual heart attack!

Our Roots—Our Hearts

In a recent *Christian Century* article a church history professor from Southern Baptist Theological Seminary in Louisville writes on "Southern Baptists: In Search of a Century." His thesis is that Southern Baptists represent a nineteenth century, white male, southern orientation. He argues that "Southern Baptists are a people shaped irrevocably by 19th century populism and folk religion."

However, as anyone knows who has lived or even visited in the South, things are much different than they were a hundred years ago. Again, the author of this article says that "with the breakdown of cultural and denominational stability, the SBC (Southern Baptist Convention) has confronted a significant dilemma: how to reconcile its 19th–century orientation with an increasingly 21st–century world. In short, the Southern Baptist Convention is a denomination in search of a century." The author concludes with a personal note: "at times...I was embarrassed to be a Southern Baptist— embarrassed because we are too white, too powerful, too southern and too cocksure that God is on our side."

The honesty of this author's reflection has provoked thinking on my part about my own denomination. Although there is some similarity for some of us Quakers to this nineteenth century Southern Baptist culture, other parts of Quakerism could not be further from this orientation! I would be tempted to say that Southern Baptists know their heart— though it may be in the past of history. We Quakers, on the other hand, are not in search of a century (history), but we are in search of our hearts. And there are many other denominations in our predicament.

It is our search for our heart that pulls Quakers—unfortunately, I think—continually to look back to the seventeenth century—our period of origin. We have idealized— and sometimes idolized—this foundational period in our history. Frequently, we are found trying unsuccessfully to recreate it in our own times. Spiritually speaking, Fox, Barclay, Penn, Fell are our heroes and heroines. The Valiant Sixty become bigger than life. And yet, if Quakers are looking for our heart, this history offers a clue: hearts are in people.

We Quakers will need to pray with the Psalmist when he petitions God: "Create in me a clean heart, O God, and put a new and right spirit within me." (Ps. 51:10) With this clean heart and new spirit we will again have people centered in God and focused on the world. We will see rising out of our midst new leaders—charismatic women and men—who will call forth a kingdom people ready for tomorrow.

In the words of an early twentieth century British Quaker, William C. Braithwaite, we know how this kingdom people will be gathered. "It is by drawing out the faculties of mind and soul that we shall multiply men of vision; it is by fellowship that we shall promote that enrichment of experience which is the special reward of friendship; it is by service that we shall express with living power the truth we hold."

This kingdom people will be a people impatient with "ism's"—even Quakerism or denominationalism! Finding our new heart will not make us "Quakers," but friends—as Jesus said, "I have called you friends." (Jn. 15:15) It will begin with me and with thee.

Finally, it is not just a Southern Baptist problem or Quaker problem—finding your heart is a human, spiritual problem. But, there is always the divine answer which solves the human problem. Join God's people—now!

Tender In Spirit

We who find ourselves regularly in the church hear much about love, compassion and caring. We are expected to love our enemies (even the one in the next pew). We are cajoled to have compassion on the hungry around the world (but little mention of those close to the golden arches of McDonalds). We are enjoined to care for the poor across town (those whom most of us identify as blacks living on "that side of town" where we do not go). I have seriously pondered why—in spite of this rhetoric—I do not always love, have compassion or care.

I have concluded that love, compassion and care are difficult or impossible without tenderness. Tenderness is a "soft" or "warm" word. Even the sound of it makes me relax. Soft and warm are characteristics of God's Spirit. A "Pharaoh's heart" is not tender. It is hard, stony and brittle. With a different metaphor, those of us who are not vegetarians know what tenderized meat offers our taste.

Soft and warm are often seen as feminine qualities. That women evidence these more frequently than men, I would allow. However, I think finally they are most appropriately seen as qualities of the Holy Spirit—which incidentally in Hebrew and Greek is a feminine word. In the Spirit, then, is a way males can join females in being tender—being soft and warm. Maybe women just simply are better at being molded by the Spirit!

To experience the transforming love of God expressed through the grace of the Holy Spirit will necessarily make us tender. If you do not become tender in this experience, it has not yet "touched" you. To have been transformed by God inevitably makes you "tender in spirit." You become a pliable instrument of God's continuing grace in the world.

To be tender in the Spirit means that you become tender in relationship to other women and men and children. Because of what God has done for you, you cannot treat anyone else as "enemy." Because of God's grace, the enemy is one for whom you have tenderness. The enemy becomes your test. If you run the enemy off the road because he passed you, you are driving with a hardened heart.

To be tender in God's Spirit means that we become capable of compassion. Compassion is an empty word until someone comes along who needs us to be tender with them. Tenderness is the assuring hand held securely. Compassion is the deep-felt, tender presence with another. In God's Spirit we can, in fact, develop tenderness for those around the world. Through prayer we can be tender towards those who have less. Through our tenderness, those who have less can legitimately ask us for part of what we have—and in compassion we will give it.

To be tender in God's Spirit means that we allow ourselves to care. To care is to risk our selfishness. To care is to realize that we are vulnerable to someone asking not only for what we have....but asking for us! To care is to begin to realize I minister—ministry which is giving myself to others. A hard and selfish person does not give, but hoards.

When you have become tender in God's Spirit, you can not possibly hoard that tenderness. You must express it in love, compassion and care. These really are kingdom qualities. God's kingdom is wrought not by might and strife but by this tenderness.

The contemporary writer, Kenneth Boulding, has written a sonnet which ends with these words, "Ah!—but what know ye, ye blind lords of strife, about the secret Kingdom of Man's life!" The tender-hearted know this secret—and are called to share it!

Encourage One Another

Over the years I have experienced sincere, helpful encouragement from a multitude of persons. Who among us does not love to see the postman walking up our walk to deliver a piece of mail. And who among us does not eagerly reach for that mail with all the hopes and expectations that not only is it "for me," but also that it be "good news." We love to hear from our friends—through the post to know we have been affirmed in who we are. A phone call or personal visit can even be better!

All of us have known people who just seem to have a gift of encouraging others. Simply to be with these people makes us feel positive about ourselves and better about our situation. These are the people who even make bad news tolerable, if not understandable. And good news they are able to communicate in marvelous ways! In this way they are like angels—bearers of good news.

What makes up "encouragement" and what makes it work? Why can some people do it so well and others are "masters of discouragement?" To answer these questions means to understand a little about the nature of encouragement. Literally, our English word comes from the French word, *encouragement.* To know this provides an investigative clue. Hiding in this French word is another French word, *coeur,* which means "heart." With the preposition en (in) plus *coeur* (heart) one can now understand that encouragement has to do with being "in the heart." To be encouraging, then, would mean to be "from the heart."

My "heart" is a shorthand way of talking about the real me—the true self. To be "in the heart " is a way of talking about being in touch with who I am and what I am. As a Christian, I realize who I am and what I am takes seriously my relationship with God. As a Christian, I am a transformed creature of God—a human whose heart has been remade in the image of God. A Christian is one who has risked the vulnerability of dying to the old self and letting Christ remake our heart. As Paul put it, "if any one is in Christ, he is a new creation; the old has passed away, behold, the new has come." (II Cor. 5:17) From this experience, it is possible specifically to talk about Christian encouragement.

Christian encouragement is what I offer "from my heart" to another person. What I offer is the truth of my being—as God through Christ in the Holy Spirit has worked and reworked me. This is my gift in encouraging others. As a child of God I can offer—encourage—that possibility in literally every other person. I can affirm them, build up and make them feel valued and valuable.

Finally, Christian encouragement does not come from a mailcarrier's delivery of a letter. Encouragement—in the Christian sense—comes from the delivery of someone's heart—literally, Christ's pouring his heart out "for me" and "for you." In his book, *The Encourager*, D. Elton Trueblood captures the essence of this angelic message. "It is a great privilege to be a human being. To be human is to share in both tragedy and wonder, and we can never express adequately the depth of either of these. One of the most exciting of human facts is that persons are able to stimulate each other in productive ways."

As encouragers, let us go into the world stimulating others in productive ways. This is our great commission! It is a mission of courage. Its commission will be encouraging.

The Surprise Of Living

There are spiritual seasons in our lives. Sometimes the spring's strong winds give way to softer, subtler summer breezes of God's Spirit. Sometimes, it even feels like there is no spiritual blowing at all—when God's movement stops and we reach a spiritual still-point. Now we are in a "dry" period.

When spiritual dryness evaporates the spiritual moisture in us, it is time seriously to return to prayer. In his book, *Quest for God*, the Jewish theologian, Abraham Joshua Heschel, offers a view of prayer for dry places. "To pray is to take notice of the wonder, to regain a sense of the mystery that animates all being, the divine margin in all attainments." To understand prayer in this fashion opens in exciting ways the whole idea of prayer. No longer is it sufficient merely to see prayer as verbalizing sentiments to God. Especially, in dry periods we usually have no words—we have developed spiritual laryngitis. Or worse, we no longer even feel "connected" with a God to whom we can speak. Here is where Heschel advises us to see "prayer is our humble *answer* to the inconceivable surprise of living."

The surprise of living! This is always the beginning point of prayer. We are reminded of Thomas Kelly's classic book, *A Testament of Devotion*: "Begin where you are. Live this present moment, this present hour as you now sit in your seats, in utter, utter submission and openness...If you slip and stumble and forget God...don't spend too much time in anguished regrets and self accusations but begin again, just where you are."

In every dry period we are yet alive! Too frequently, what happens is we become "dead" to the surprise of our living. We become so numbed by our own being that we take ourselves for granted. As a lover of ourselves, we have now jilted our "self." To pray is once more to take notice of our wonder. Our own lives are signs of a larger wonder in the world. It is there—in you and me. All we have to do is take notice.

To take notice of wonder is simply the art of paying attention. In *Soul Making* Alan Jones surmises "the holding in of the energy in simple attention gives birth to something new. The soul comes into being." This new-born soul—from the dry deadness—is once again awakened to the wonder of the human body, to appreciate the human mind—to value the smile and be moved by the tear. To pay attention is to refuse to trash our treasure. To take notice of wonder is to relocate God—the creative source of life and the recreative resource of the surprise of living. This is an awe some prayer.

This awesome prayer, located in wonder, enables us, secondly, to regain a sense of the *mystery* which animates all beings. In dry places we lose that sense—we feel like nothing is happening, nothing matters. There is a kind of spiritual boredom settling on our spirits. This boredom emaciates the face of living—it erases any "mystery" life has to offer. Boredom is loss of spirit, loss of animation. It is like going to the movie when the reel stops and figures on the screen slide to their bizarre halt. With the loss of the animating mystery, prayer ceases and complaining commences. Wonder turns wimpish and mystery becomes misery.

To regain the mystery of God is to feel again the animation of life. Heschel says, "suddenly we feel ashamed of our clashes and complaints in the face of the tacit glory in nature." In her book, *The Healing Light*, Agnes Sanford discloses something of this loving mystery of God. "We become perfected in love by trying to do it. This method is so simple that any child can learn it. It is merely to connect in spirit with love of God, send that love to the other person, and see him re-created in goodness and joy and peace." Love re-creates us in our dry places by enabling us to feel the movement of God's Spirit animating our beings.

The animation of our souls puts us, thirdly, in the place to see the divine *margin* in all attainments. This is to be in that place of knowing—knowing which infuriates a world bent on its own course. In Graham Green's novel, *The Power and the Glory*, an atheistic lieutenant incarnates this infuriating spirit. Greene writes, "it infuriated him to think that there were still people in the state who believed in a loving and merciful God. There are mystics who are said to have experienced God directly."

The mystic is not only the one taken to the third heaven. More generally, the mystic is the one taken into the divine margin. There we know the grace of care and the gift of love. In that divine margin we learn prayer is the rain which falls in dry seasons—bringing the soul back to its green lushness. In the aridity of separation from God's love, the soul withers. In the garden of the divine margin, the soul springs back to life.

Hildegard of Bingen, a thirteenth century Flemish Beguine, describes this freshness. "You will find the newness of heaven...in your heart and the newness of life—giving the breath of life—in your spirit." Dry times are opportunities for newness of life. There God will always come again to move and breath life into us. Take a deep breath—and live!

Chapter 7
Places of Nurture

Alone With God

Solitude means to be alone. But, often we are afraid of being alone. The fear of solitude is the fear of loneliness. Loneliness is a real fear because the threat is that there truly might be no "other" present—or potentially present—to me. Loneliness is a disease-like experience which afflicts old and young alike.

Loneliness threatens us at our deepest level—our most human desire is to love and be loved. Loneliness means there is no possibility to love— because there is no one to love. Solitude, then, as part of our religious discipline feels risky. To choose to be alone always risks being lonely.

Henri Nouwen has helped me to understand and appreciate and practice solitude—being by myself. Nouwen writes in *The Way of the Heart* "solitude is the furnace of transformation. Without solitude we remain victims of our society and continue to be entangled in the illusions of the false self." This has been an important knowing for myself as I came to realize how much of my "self" is developed and nurtured to please the "other." My false self shows up all over the place. I wear a tie to be acceptable. I repress anger to be likeable. I fake interest when the other is uninteresting. I am assuring when I should be challenging. I am funny when I should be serious. I am aloof when I need to be present.

This is precisely the "self" which needs to be transformed in God's furnace. This is the old self, which the apostle Paul says, must be seen to death in order to allow the new self to emerge. It is precisely in this threat of death to my "self" that I most acutely feel the anxiety of loneliness. In his book, *The Inner Loneliness*, Sebastian Moore puts this "inner loneliness" in an understandable context when he describes loneliness as being "that I am, and nobody cares...the center of the lonely 'I am' is an infinite insecurity."

Moore further suggests that only God can meet us in this inner loneliness. Only God can dispel our fears that ultimately loneliness will remain—that haunting fear that ultimately I *will be alone*. It will be God—in Christ—who truly becomes not only "Other" but "friend" to us. This friend will love *us*, —purely and simply *us*—not for what we do or how we act. Those will be important, but ultimately because God is love, God loves me and God loves you.

Nouwen gives us some words by which we begin to understand how we profit by our solitude, our being alone. He declares "we enter into solitude first of all to meet our Lord and to be with him and him alone. Our primary task in solitude, therefore, is not to pay undue attention to the many faces which assail us, but to keep the eyes of our mind and heart on him who is our divine savior. Only in the context of grace can we face our sin; only in the place of healing do we dare to show our wounds; only with a single-minded attention to Christ can we give up our clinging fears and face our own true nature."

When Jesus is seen in this context—as Lord—we can sing anew, "What a friend we have in Jesus." He is the ultimate friend who meets us in our solitude and loves us. He allays the anxiety of our future and slays the fear of loneliness. In his book, *Jesus the Christ*, Walter Kasper tells us why Jesus is this ultimate friend. It is because "in Jesus we finally come face to face with God."

And so, ironically solitude takes us to the ultimate place of relationship!

Sense The Freshness Of God

One of the best smells in the world is the freshness after a rain. Frequently, I think the Spirit of God washes over us like a rain and refreshes our spirits. Sadly, however, Christians often do not associate our five senses with spirituality. All our talk about the inward, spiritual journey frequently leads to a "spiritualization"—a move which robs God's Spirit of earthly, bodily media for revelation and enjoyment.

So, when we experience the raining of God's fresh drops, we might begin to open our noses for those new smells. In a marvelous passage it is suggested metaphorically that even God—the real God—employs these senses. At one point Deuteronomy talks about the time the Israelites will go into the promised land. Prophetically, the author describes how the people will "blow it" and, instead, be sent among people who "serve gods of wood and stone, the work of men's hands." (Dt. 4:28) The Deuteronomist characterizes these idols in "lifeless" ways. They "neither see, nor hear, nor eat, nor smell." To be alive is to see, to hear, to eat, and to smell. When we give up idolatrous ways and come into the real presence of God, there will be a God to see—a God who speaks. There will be a God who feeds us and, finally, a God who is fragrant.

George Fox, founder of Quakerism, knew something about this ability to smell afresh. In celebrated words describing his vision when being taken up into the paradise of God, Fox uses sensory language. "Now was I come up in spirit through the flaming sword into the paradise of God. All things were new, and all the creation gave another smell unto me than before, beyond what words can utter." Frequently, we associate visions with "seeing" and that is appropriate. But in this case, Fox powerfully aligns vision with a sense of smell. He asserts in paradise—that is, where God is— things will "smell" differently because all things are new. For Fox, all things are new because he had been "renewed up into the image of God by Christ Jesus."

Perceptively, this links our ability to smell with the image of God. Things smell new—smell fresh—when we are renewed in the image of God. All of us are created in the divine image. But predictably and unfortunately, as we go our own way, we lose touch with this image—often because we went the wrong way. In practical terms, thinking about God's image from the perspective of smell is helpful.

Appropriately, we begin with smell because smell uses the organ by which we breathe. Creation begins with God's breathing life into the first human being. Breath—the spirit—is God's continuing gift. In her book, *Prayer and Our Bodies,* Flora Slosson Wuellner says "our deep, instinctive taking of breath is receiving again the gift of life from God for each moment." A practical spirituality not only affirms that God's presence is as real as breathing, but helps us discover and develop the ability to live well. Wuellner offers advice on the first step. She suggests, "when receiving God's gifts and nurture through the senses, it is essential to be deliberate, aware, focusing upon each event, receptive to each sensory experience in its uniqueness."

A practical spirituality helps us detect the refreshing rains of God's Spirit by focusing and developing a "deliberate awareness." Take a moment now—where you are—and become aware of your breathing. Shut your eyes, be quiet and find the rhythm of your breathing. Conscious of that, now become aware of any smells. If you are inside, or in a familiar place, usually you are unaware of smell just as you are unaware of breathing.

After some time, go outside and smell. When you go into the country, there are wonderful smells, new-mown hay and ploughed fields. Go to the kitchen to inhale the scent of baking bread or of fresh-cut watermelon. Our microwave life-styles are robbing us of chances to linger with the smell.

This is not to say microwaves are bad; indeed, they make life easier but that does not necessarily mean better. With time saved, we will have to find our smells elsewhere.

It is with our microwave life-styles that spirituality must become concerned. We live life fast—efficiently—and often meaninglessly. Real life has an odor. Odor comes from the Latin, *odor,* meaning "smell, scent, perfume, ointment, stench." This last word, stench, gives an important clue for a second step in practical spirituality. To enter into God's place with its new smell usually requires dealing with the stinky stuff!

If our spiritual sniffers are numbed by inattention or have become diseased through neglect, then we will have to start here. As Fox reminds us, we get rid of the stink by being renewed up into God's image. Wuellner recognizes that "most of us are still wounded, frightened people needing inner healing." Too many of us have chosen a deodorant instead of healing. We need the touch of God's gentle rain. Through the renewing work of God—through prayer and other spiritual disciplines—we can begin to catch the scent of the divine.

Try using incense with prayer. Sit in a garden while praying. Now metaphorically begin to smell the odor of your life. Imagine the stinky places refreshed with the divine rain. Imagine the dirt of life washed away. Imagine the stink fading way. Thus transformed, you will come to be a perfume in a world of pollutants. You will become God's ointment—anointing others with your sweet-smelling fragrance.

Our bodies—earthly and spiritual—become the medium for God's wonderful presence. Imagine that!

Fire Of Love

At the Christmas season in 1980 Richard Newby wrote the preface to a book entitled, *Life is to be Celebrated.* Now some years later Richard, a friend, is dead. Richard's first book of sermons had been given the title, *Spiritual Fire and Other Messages* (1977). The image of spiritual fire has been an important gift from Richard to me and others. Religious symbolism employs fire both widely and powerfully to describe experiences of the spiritual medium.

No doubt those of us who celebrate the Advent–Christmas season read again and again the familiar words of John the Baptist. As preparation for the coming of God's messiah, John proclaimed that "I baptize you with water for repentance, but he who is coming after me...will baptize you with the Holy Spirit and with fire." (Mt. 3:11) As an image, fire generally has two functions: destructive and purifying. In this instance, it will be useful to focus on the purifying function of fire. As we shall see, this often is another way to talk about love.

In the fourteenth century an English hermit, Richard Rolle, wrote a treatise entitled *The Fire of Love*. In this splendid piece Rolle uses the image of fire to describe love. This gives us a clue to understand something about the nature of life purified in Christ's fire, namely, the "fired Christian" becomes a "lover." Rolle also helps us understand something about the process of becoming a Christian who loves. He uses fire as a metaphor for love because fire both *burns* and *illumines.*

Just as a log placed on the fire is transformed, so the fire of the Holy Spirit, according to Rolle, "really seizes the heart, burns it up entirely and changes it, as if in a fire, and brings it back into that form which is most like God." So, the initial stage in learning about love is to be burned! We must "fire" the old self, be transformed and be opened to the other—

to God and neighbor. Only in this *transformation* is the possibility presented that we can then *conform* to Christ's love.

The basis of conforming to Christ's love comes in the second stage of being fired, namely, as the fire illumines. In this sense, fire as a symbol parallels the image of light. In light we realize that darkness is eradicated; in fire we experience the coldness giving way to warmth and heat. We can push the symbolism further and acknowledge that coldness represents death and warmth signifies life.

We confess that the fire of the Holy Spirit empowers us to feel who we are and where we are going. We recognize ourselves to be friends of Jesus and friends of Jesus' friends. Being fired by the Holy Spirit is recognizing that to be alive is to be loved and to love. In this, Richard Newby was correct: life is to be celebrated.

A celebrated life is a life which knows God, experiences the burning, illumining fire of God and is moved into the fellowship of God's lovers. Truly, this calls for celebration!

Rivers Of Living Water

God's universe, of which we occupy only an insignificant place on this earth, truly is wondrous. We can continue to be amazed at how rain can turn to snow, how water can become ice or steam. Those physical changes suggest something of the nature of the miraculous. Christmas is part of cyclical seasons which liturgically celebrates a miracle— a miracle in which we affirm a baby to be the divine entree into this world. It is always easier to perceive the miraculous at a special time like Christmas.

Christmas is the season of new beginnings; sacramentally, it is akin to baptism—that place where people liturgically use water to symbolize new birth and the gift of the Spirit. Water is typical of the "ordinary" becoming the medium for the miraculous. By itself, water is an ordinary piece of our daily reality which makes our life—well, livable!

In the teaching of Jesus, water was not only seen literally as necessary for life, but became the symbol for abundant life. In his book, *When the Well Runs Dry*, Thomas H. Green tells us "Jesus lived in a world where water was a much more precious commodity. Not only was it scarce, but much of what was available was dangerous...For him and for his people, the value of water—good water, flowing water, what Jesus called 'living' water—was very great." Jesus' symbolic use of water for "abundant life" follows from his Jewish heritage.

The prophet Isaiah pens beautiful words describing God's redemptive presence for Israel. God declares, "I am doing a new thing; now it springs forth, do you not perceive it? I will make a way in the wilderness and rivers in the desert...for I give water in the wilderness, rivers in the desert..." (Isa. 43:19-20) Later, God elaborates. "I will pour water on the thirsty land, and streams on the dry ground; I will pour my Spirit upon your descendants, and my blessings on your offspring." (Isa. 44:3) God's Spirit is like the water in a river—available to the dry ground of the soul to moisten the clay of our being and germinate the Seed planted therein.

If we pause at the river of the Spirit to let it speak metaphorically, there is much it will whisper when we listen. The river is almost always moving. Some small creeks can dry up—or usually dry up—in the summer season. But with rain, they spring to life. Rivers can run fast or meander slowly. Rivers are always directed, they are moving somewhere. They also have a *source* from which their life springs. And so, metaphorically, the river of the Spirit originates in God and flows into the world which is God's world.

For the one in the world who sets out on the spiritual journey—that one will always come to a river. Jesus came to the Jordan and received the Spirit. We come to the river of Jesus and receive the same Spirit. The fourth gospel has Jesus proclaim, "if any one thirsts, let him come to me and drink. He who believes in me, as the scriptures has said, 'out of his heart shall flow rivers of living water.' Now this he said about the Spirit, which those who believed in him were to receive." (Jn. 7:37-39)

God in Jesus is the source of the rivers of living water which flow into our hearts. We will experience the movement of this in our inner being and will pour it out sacramentally in our outward actions. Our spiritual rivers are directed in ministry. We will be called spiritually to water God's earth.

Our sacramental presence in this will be just like the baby at Christmas. Even though physically we occupy only an insignificant place on this planet in the midst of a huge galaxy in a larger universe, we continue to be wondrous and miraculous signs of a higher power. In a world parched with meaninglessness, our miracle is not an invitation to get wet, but an invitation for people to step into our rivers.

We offer the river of life—the source of abundant life. Come and live!

Come And Worship

Writing about worship Rufus Jones said, "by worship I mean the act of rising to a personal, experimental consciousness of the real presence of God which floods the soul with joy and bathes the whole inward spirit with refreshing streams of life." No one who feels the fresh winds of God's Spirit can fail to worship in this sense. And when there are not fresh winds of God's Spirit, worship may not have taken place even though the institutional church declares, "Worship at 11:00 a.m.!"

Rather than offering "worship" at an appointed hour, we do well to recognize worship as "the act of rising to a personal, experimental consciousness" of God. Even though we may "go" to worship, we have not thereby "worshiped." As a Quaker, I can scoff at those churches who sacramentally use outward elements for communion. I can feel a kind of smugness in seeing those folks assume simply because the priest says the words, "This is my body," somehow miraculously and momentarily the wafer becomes Christ's body. "No way," I am inwardly tempted to chuckle.

And yet, do I, as a Quaker, not run the same risk when I can habitually say, "I have been to worship?" Actually, on many Sundays I might more correctly admit that around 11:00 a.m. I entered an architectural edifice (sometimes identified as a church, or more Quakerly, a "meetinghouse"). At the time, feeling out of sorts and generally grumpy (or add your own descriptor: angry, tired, bored, etc.), I went through the motions (of sitting in silence or through a program, it matters not!). Relieved when it was over and having received nothing from it, I adjourned to the nearest restaurant for coffee and sweet rolls—affirming to the waiter that I had been to worship!

Actually, Rufus Jones has a splendid antidote to this kind of "non-worship." Rightly, he says, worship is an experience of meeting God. It is not sufficient merely to affirm that worship is an experience; the person now having coffee earlier had an experience, but it was not one of meeting God.

As Jones would say, "there is one act of life which does bring us in a special and peculiar way into the holy of holies of religion...this central act is worship." The shift to the image of the temple is helpful. We can go to the temple—even enter it—but that is not yet worship. Indeed, we must enter the holy of holies—for there is where God is "found." Here is the sacred spot—sacred because that is where God's presence is felt. For us, this sacred spot is our heart—the inner sanctuary. Worship is meeting God here.

In rather touching, sacramental language Jones suggests what entering this temple of the heart is like. It is to come to what he calls an experience of God which floods the soul with joy. Could it be this is how one should understand worship—as a baptismal event? We go to designated places—the heart—with other spiritual pilgrims and hope to get flooded! We enter our holy of holies—the inner sanctuary—and there wait for the divine flood of joy. For this flood of joy we need no ark because our joy buoys us on the divine waters.

There is no drowning—only living in these waters. The intention for worship is the expectation that joy will flood over us, anointing us with a fresh Spirit. Jones continues the sacramental perspective, noting this personal encounter with God in worship "bathes the whole inward spirit with refreshing streams of life." The fresh winds of God's Spirit now become the refreshing streams of life. We are nourished by these streams. Who can fail to think of the Psalmist talking about the person who delights in the law of the Lord, for that one "is like a tree planted by streams of water, that yields its fruit in its season, and its leaf does not wither." (Ps. 1:3)

In an odd kind of way, there is a spiritual law for worship. Simply put, it would say the one who does not worship, does not know God. Metaphorically, this law would stipulate the one who does not worship will become a dying tree—dying because the streams of water have subsided. The Jewish theologian, Abraham Joshua Heschel, knew this. He said, "how grateful I am to God that there is a duty to worship, a law to remind my distraught mind that it is time to think of God, time to disregard my ego for at least a moment!"

Ah, but there is our modern problem: time to disregard my ego for at least a moment! You have to be kidding! Too many of us have confused our ego and our heart. We do well to recall the words of Jones when he declared worship to be the experience of God's presence which floods the soul and bathes the spirit. Pride is a flooded ego and greed is a bathed ego. Common to both pride and greed is my ego.

True worship humbles my pride and impoverishes my greed. In worship I recognize I am not god, but I am God's. Now, I am free for joy and the refreshing streams of life. With my ego out of the way, I am free genuinely to worship. With clarity, I can say I am not going *to* worship. I am going to *worship*—the central act of my life.

Hallelujah!

There Is Life In The Desert

One does not need to be very perceptive to be aware of the immense amount of sadness in the world. One can walk through a department store and see very few evidences of happiness. One can strike up an innocent conversation at the gas station and have disappointment, anger and melancholy come pouring out. We can look deep in our own souls and see our shortcomings, experience our failures and know our own sadness.

There is always as much—or probably more—sadness as happiness in holiday seasons. Sadness results from broken relationships, failed hopes and fractured dreams. There truly are reasons in my life and in the world to be sad. There is misfortune beyond our control and disasters beyond any decency. These are what might be called "legitimate" sorrows or sadness. The loss of a parent or loved one is truly reason for sadness and requires a grieving process.

However, there are other forms and expressions of sadness which may be "illegitimate." Those would be the sadness of not being Miss America or getting rich! To be in sadness over this type of experience may, in fact, point to our participation in a kind of death. How can we purge ourselves of this ineffectual sorrow?

By going to the desert! In his book, *Soul Making*, Alan Jones tells us desert believers "understand that there is no real loving without tears." Tears do go with sadness and sorrow. But what does love have to do with sadness? In one sense, we can say "Everything." True love will mean we know fully "our-self." Fully to know our-self will mean giving up the false images of who we are—what we want to become. It means laying aside the grand illusions of our omnipotence—or impotence. It means laying aside that on our own we are great—or awful.

Loving means going into the desert of our "self" to discover "this empty space is actually indescribably full. It is a kind of dying, because it means giving up the manipulative concepts we have about ourselves and (worse, if you are a believer) our 'God.' A kind of 'atheism' sets in with regard to the infantile 'God' of our immature imagination." In this personal desert there will be some dying—and the requisite grieving. But, this dying puts us in touch with the re-birthing which, finally, will deliver us out of sadness into vitality.

This is because in this silence—in this desert—Jones suggests, we will be found by God as God truly is. This God will bring the rebirth out of our death—bring us to become the person God created us to be and desires us into that new possibility. This is not to be Miss America or successful in worldly ways, but to become a follower of Christ. To follow Christ will lead us to be happy in the Lord and a lover in Christ's name.

We can be appropriately sad for a world which does not yet know the true source of happiness. But, there is a secret which Hannah Whitall Smith discovered in her book, *The Christian's Secret of a Happy Life*, and shared at the outset of that classic. "Then for the first time I saw, as in a flash, that the religion of Christ ought to be, and was meant to be, to its possessors, not something to make them miserable, but something to make them happy."

Together let us celebrate this "happy birth-day!"

Settled Or Directed

Many of us are creatures of habit. We develop the taste for the same foods, we do things at the same time and, psychologically, we take comfort in life's predictabilities. There is a level of comfort which routine and regularity afford. This level of comfort often is experienced as a sense of *security*. To be secure is to feel safe, healthy and at ease. Certainly, all of these qualities are positive and sought by the majority of us. Many of us have been rich with comfort, security and health. But, richness often has a problematic side.

The problem with this richness is twofold. In the first place, we have a nagging concern that not all humans have been as richly endowed. Seen from afar, Third World countries usually are devoid of all three gifts of security, comfort and health. To know this causes us some uneasiness— even if we intend to ignore it! Secondly, and closer to home, we know of folks in our own proximity who are not comfortable, who are not safe and who are diseased. "There but for the grace of God go I," we can shudder. And so, in spite of our efforts to "settle into" our comfort, security and health—to become habituated with our richness—we experience an underlying, haunting unsettledness.

It is precisely in my experience of unsettledness that I have been blessed with a chance—bequeathed with an opportunity—for something more special than comfort, security or health can offer in their own right. Ironically, this something special is God. In my experience, to know God is to come to know something potentially about direction in life—direction which challenges any feeling or desire simply to be settled into the comforts of life.

What I now realize is the subtle—but significant—difference between being *settled* and being *directed*. To know God is to be called into a place where the Spirit of God will direct us. God's Spirit does direct! Typically, spiritual direction has an unsettling effect because it challenges and changes us. We experience ourselves being called out of our old habits—our routine is frequently disrupted and our regularities become re-woven. We are called forth from ourselves—from a "comfort" self to a self which is obedient.

To be thus directed means we experience movement. With a discovered sense of focus, direction offers the only chance to become the person whom God wants us to be. To choose direction rather than to be settled is to recognize the essential *dynamism* of life—and to have a prayer that our lives are moving meaningfully towards the only real goal there is: God. To be directed is to realize our destiny.

Alan Jones puts it triumphantly when he says "you are destined for something beyond your dying, and that destination is part of who you are right now. However old you are, however cynical you may have become, however diminished that Flame may be within you, you are destined for God."

This is such good news that most of us can scarcely believe it. And so, we spend a lifetime of wandering—of being misdirected and misguided—because we can not come to believe that we have a destiny and that is to be with God—that indeed we can be on fire for life!

But...it is true!

Chapter 8
Grace

Kingdom Living

In his book, *Leaving Home*, Garrison Keillor tells an ironical story of Daryl and his dad. It was dad's failure to make plans or keep from changing his mind which drove Daryl crazy. Those formative years trained Daryl for one thing, as Keillor narrates;" they raised him to bear up under hardship and sadness and disappointment and disaster, but what if you're brought up to be a stoic and your life turns out lucky...?" This is the irony: you prepare for the worst "and life is lovely to you—what then? You're ready to endure trouble and pain, and instead God sends you love—what do you do?"

What do we do? Daryl's story is nothing less than a lesson of grace. The trouble with grace is that it always messes up plans and preparations for disaster! Some of us work so hard at life that grace can neither be expected nor trusted—even if it comes! Stoically, we form life to prepare for the hardship and the sadness. Around every corner of life we square our shoulders to withstand the blast of disappointments. We hunker down under the weight of disasters. But, what happens if God turns out to be graceful?

"But," we retort, "what about all those disasters in the world and in my life? What about the pain and sadness?" For us spiritual stoics, grace seems to be either naivete—foolish. Or, grace is a lack of realism concerning what life is really all about. We who are spiritually stoic want quickly to point to Jesus and the cross. For us, the cross symbolizes disaster; it brought death. And now, when the spiritual stoic hears Jesus' words, "Follow me," that person also hears the familiar preceding words, to deny ourselves and take up own crosses. (Mk. 8:34) So, our understanding forms our expectations...and our expectations usually determine our future.

Maybe, we who are spiritual stoics have misunderstood the cross. Maybe, we have stood on the wrong side of it—even while believing it! We do well to go back to Paul's saying, "the word of the cross is folly to those who are perishing, but to us who are being saved it is the power of God." (I Cor. 1:18) The word of the cross is not damnation but salvation.

The power of the cross is grace, the realization that we have prepared for the worst—and life turns out to be lovely! The hope of the cross is that the stoic who prepares to endure trouble and pain discovers instead that God sends us love.

"But," we retort," Jesus calls us to be disciples not Pollyannas. Pollyanna, you know, is optimistically naive." We spiritual stoics are a hard lot! We become very committed to our expectations,—so much so, we better watch out. Expectations are the way we live our life-plans. They are the way we look at life and by which we receive it as the future becoming present. Expectation comes from the Latin, *exspecto,* which itself is a compound word of *ex* ("out of, from") and *specto* ("to look at, aim at"). Expectations, then, are the ways our "eyes" are conditioned to see God, ourselves and our world.

Too many of us have "bad eyes" because our expectations are messed up. God re-conditions us through grace—which is the way God transforms our expectations. Grace is always that realization that God sends us love. Love is the invitation to relationship and the means of realizing the kingdom. Especially, those of us who go to church need to be reminded of the difference between the church and the kingdom. Howard Snyder, in his book, *Liberating the Church,* says "the church gets in trouble whenever it thinks it is in the church business rather than the kingdom business." He continues by showing how easy it is to get on the wrong side of the cross. "Church people think about how to get people into the church; Kingdom people think about how to get the church into the world. Church people worry that the world might change the church; Kingdom people work to see the church change the world."

Jesus invites us to turn the corners of our lives—not with squared shoulders for the blast of disasters—but with relaxed expectations for the grace of God's Spirit. Through Jesus, God transforms our expectations. Through the transforming grace, we are given the kingdom-plan, the fruits of which are peace and joy.

The kingdom-plan is not an invitation to naivete, but to newness. This newness is a sense of peace. That peace can keep us centered—in spite of whatever frenzy we create or freakishness the world delivers. The kingdom-plan is not Pollyannish, but powerful. This power is grounded in a sense of joy. It is a joy which knows what to do when God sends us love.

En-joy it!

History Shapes Us

Having spent significant time one summer in Oxford, England, I would share some observations on history. History is both the narration of events, as well as the interpretation of those events. History is worth knowing simply because it is *interesting*. However, history becomes important to know when it becomes *meaningful*. When history is meaningful, the past both forms and shapes our present. Let me illustrate both aspects of history—its interest and its meaning—as one walks from Oxford City Centre to a flat where I lived.

In the summer Oxford is a busy, crowded city with a multiplicity of languages and colors of the peoples of the world. You will get bumped as we leave the city heading for the village of Woodstock, where the future Queen Elizabeth was residing when hearing about Mary's death. She set out in 1558 for London and to begin a long and crucial reign as monarch (until 1603). To talk about Queen Elizabeth prepares us for our first historical visit.

Just at the north edge of the old city of Oxford you stop before a monument. It is called the "Martyrs' Monument" and was erected almost three centuries later—in 1841. You can look up to see in stone three life-size men. You begin to read these words of dedication:

> To the glory of God and in grateful commemoration of his servants, Thomas Cranmer, Nicholas Ridley, Hugh Latimer, prelates of the Church of England, who near this spot yielded their bodies to be burned, bearing witness to the sacred truths which they had affirmed and maintained against the errors of the church of Rome, and rejoicing that to them it was given not only to believe in Christ but also to surrender for his sake.

These three men were Anglican priests who, in 1555/6, were martyred under Queen "Bloody Mary." This history is *interesting* because it says so much about sixteenth century England—and the subsequent formation of the Church of England. But so far as I can tell, for most people—British and non-British alike—this monument presently narrates no meaningful history. For the most part, it is now a roosting place for pigeons and a place for foreign teen-agers to sit. For these teen-agers, perhaps, this monument tells of three men being killed—and, for them, it is not even interesting history!

Five minutes up Woodstock Road brings you to a plain red door leading into the local Quaker meeting. In the library we can read a Journal—the Journal being a different kind of monument. In George Fox's seventeenth century *Journal* again you encounter historical Oxford. In a 1647 entry George says that "the Lord opened to me that being bred at Oxford or Cambridge was not enough to fit and qualify men to be ministers of Christ." This religious history becomes interesting because of the significant shift it evidences from the previous century of Cranmer, Latimer and Ridley. But more than interesting, the history of Fox and Quakers is *meaningful* because it impacts me personally, as well as contemporary Quakerism. Historically, it says something about the nature of ministry which Quakers—in contradistinction to some other Christian bodies—still presently affirm: that being smart or well-bred does not qualify one for ministry. Quakers are historical and contemporary witnesses (monuments?) to the truth that all kinds of people—women, as well as men—farmers as well as Oxford dons—are ministers.

This interesting *and* meaningful history is worth learning because it will continue to shape and fashion the Christian future. It will form saintly people who, like Cranmer, Ridley and Latimer, will yield their bodies as servants of God. In fact, *we are God's monuments* ! We are different than the Martyrs' Monument because we are still mobile—still walking the streets of Oxford or New York.

As history-makers, we are given the opportunity yet to witness to "that of God in every person" and, thus, help those we meet to create a meaningful life. To become history-makers in this sense will require a conversion—just as it required conversions of Cranmer, Latimer, Ridley and George Fox. In his book, *Biography as Theology*, James Wm. McLendon, Jr. writes "conversions are not so much the introduction of new elements into the self, as they are the rearrangement of elements already present, the shifting of the center of gravity; for the 'new' elements were present before the conversion, and the 'old' elements are still present after."

Our conversion will make us a monument—interesting and meaningful. Stand tall! Tell your story!

A Ride Downtown

Once a month I make an uncomfortable drive through downtown Richmond, IN. Oh, the drive is not uncomfortable because of a lousy car; actually I have a very nice car! Bumpy roads are not the problem either. Actually, the city has only recently freshly paved the road so that it is a very smooth thoroughfare. The problem is I must make the drive past the county courthouse—the place where folks on welfare are waiting—a crowd with what seems like mostly mothers of youngsters and, who themselves, seem so young. It is worse as the winter months approach. Rain makes me feel even worse; snow is the pits. "But for the grace of God, there I am," I have often thought. But what and how does this have to do with grace?

It is not fair to wonder why a grace–ful God would allow there to be poor, to permit the destitute to be but not to have. Rather, what we have to ask is how we, as God's servants and God's instruments on earth, can go past the courthouse—to go through life—without responding—except for maybe feeling sorry? "But, I pay taxes which support these folks," I can meekly reply.

In America there certainly is no denying that our taxes not only help build bombs but also help pay for those less materially fortunate than we are. One seems good while the other—building bombs—appears not good. But, I reason, at least the tax money is a way of sharing some of my resources. At least, those less materially fortunate have something of mine. "But, what more does the Lord require," I wonder?

What I begin to realize is that the world—and especially the poor—need not only our sharing, but they need our caring. I can share a few coins of my earnings, but do I share anything of myself? Do I care? What would it look like not to drive through or past that part of life, but to stop and start to care? Oh, I do not mean literally to stop on the street, but to slow down my life and be available to care and to listen and to attend to hurts and let them begin to attend to my needs. This could be the beginning of a new ministry. In ministry, we often will realize that we have been ministered unto!

What I know is that I have a passion for the poor or weak. This passion, however, quickly burns itself out as I drive past and do not allow the passion to generate any heat leading to action. The question for me—and maybe others—is how this "passion for" becomes "compassion"—passion with and alongside? Compassion means coming to stand with the other, to be an advocate for their needs and encourager of their wants. It means an openness and vulnerability to them—as they are—and to me—just as I am.

I begin to realize a grace–ful God may intervene in history to change the situation by changing me. In that sense, I am the poor one, the one in need of caring and compassion. I am so well off, I cannot afford to let God mess up my life! My passions must be controlled lest they become compassion. I am unwilling to have a little shared because I do not want to have to care for so much.

Jesus addressed a rich man by telling the disciples that "it is easier for a camel to go through the eye of a needle than for a rich man to enter the kingdom of God." (Mt. 19:24) To the rich man Jesus had said, "if you would be perfect, go sell what you possess and give to the poor, and you will have treasure in heaven; and come, follow me." (Mt. 19:21) Actually, to follow Jesus will mean a whole relearning process for most of us. Maybe one way to begin this relearning process of entering the kingdom of God is to begin work on what it means to give to the poor—in friendship to learn compassion instead of practicing condemnation.

Ok—let's go for a drive downtown!

'Vanity Of Vanities

Most of us want to believe in a theology of grace, but there is a nagging crumminess in our lives which makes a "gracious God" remote from our experience. Not only do we feel failed by grace, but faith itself seems as distinct as the oasis of a dessert. We may come close to an oasis—not sure whether it is real or the trick of mirage. This kind of faith will need to be tested before we can know more than the superficial "trust and obey."

Key to our testing is the appreciation of faith's role. In his book, *New Seeds of Contemplation*, Thomas Merton perceptively notes "faith incorporates the unknown into our everyday life in a living, dynamic and actual manner." For Merton the "unknown" is where our faith will be tested. "Trust and obey" simply is not sufficient in the face of the unknown. Rather, Merton suggests "faith is not just conformity, it is life. It embraces all the realms of life, penetrating into the most mysterious and inaccessible depths not only of our unknown spiritual being but even of God's own hidden essence and love. Faith, then, is the only way of opening up the true depths of reality, even of our own reality." With these words we have a clue how to engage our crumminess.

The Hebrew Bible gives philosophical words to this human crumminess. The preacher, Qoheleth, opens Ecclesiastes with the well-known words, "Vanity of vanities...vanity of vanities! All is vanity!" (Ecc. 1:2) Qoheleth continues to catalog the futility of it all: work, life and death. He moans, "what has been is what will be, and what has been done is what will be done; and there is nothing new under the sun." (Ecc. 1:9) Qoheleth concludes, "I have seen everything under the sun; and behold, all is vanity and a striving after wind." (Ecc. 1:14)

We all have experiences of vanity. Often, what is not understood is the non-spiritual quality of vanity! To grapple with vanity perhaps is to realize— for many of us—Qoheleth is absolutely correct: "All is vanity!" BUT, a theology of grace counters: "It does not have to be...and maybe, God does not want it all to be vanity!"

The *Didache*, a document from the early second century church, opens with these words: "There are two ways, one of Life and one of Death, and there is a great difference between the two ways." This classic quotation points not only to the truth of the Christian insight—there is *a way of life*—but also posits the appropriate context to understand vanity. Finally, vanity is a way of death.

Vanity comes from the Latin, *vanue*, and means "empty, vain, pointless, delusive." A vanity, then, means that in which I put faith—invest hope and engender love—cannot possibly yield fruit—precisely because it is empty. Vanity is always a loser because finally it is "nothing." It is empty and pointless. Even if some were to accuse us, "you are vain," that means they see us as puffed up with pride or self-importance—or that our sense of beauty is out of line. Vanity really means our self-perception—or, their perceptions—is misplaced. Finally, our vanity will lead to our death.

As a way of death, vanity has a clear road. We are "set up" to lose! Because we are vain, an inevitable process begins. The first stop on the vain road is *disappointment*. At some point, vanity always is punctured. My beauty may be altered. My riches may be lost—or not matter any more. Vanity always leads to disappointment. Often, our disappointment is masked by anger and we lash out.

Secondly, over a period of time and on the heels of disappointment, our vanity grows into a kind of *despondency*. Here our vanity is being exposed for what it is—illusion. Often, despondency turns into violence and we try to destroy that which has exposed us.

Finally, our vain road takes us all the way to *despair*. We slip into a place where the emptiness of vanity leaves us with no hope. Despair is a living death—no hope, no desire, no future. Vanity always will kill our "ego," but our true self is more than our ego. With God's grace, there is life.

Grace sets us on the way of life. This way brings us to a land of plenty. *Plenus* is the Latin for "plenty:" it is the opposite of vanity's emptiness. On this plentiful road we are no longer disappointed, but now become excited. This graceful way erases despondency and restores hope. As gift, life destroys despair and releases joy.

All is not vanity—but we will not know this until our vanity is gracefully killed and abundant life is revealed. Come—walk the way of life!

Outrageous Grace

"There is therefore now no condemnation for those who are in Christ Jesus. For the law of the Spirit of life in Christ Jesus has set me free from the law of sin and death." (Rom. 8:1-2) These words from the pen of the apostle Paul commence that noble eighth chapter in Romans which features Christian life in the Spirit. The chapter begins with a note describing our freedom in the Spirit and concludes by assuring us that in this freedom there is nothing "to separate us from the love of God in Christ Jesus our Lord." (Rom. 8:39) The Spirit is rightly seen as the topic of this eloquent chapter, but Spirit-living is not possible apart from the radical work of grace. The actuality of God's Spirit in our lives is the result of the choice God has made for us—in grace we have come to be in Christ Jesus and, therefore, are free from condemnation and free for the love of God.

When we come right down to it, grace is really an outrageous doctrine! Grace is that divine message which assures us of the one thing we could hope for—but often (usually?) will not allow ourselves to live for—namely, that we have been *accepted.* Grace is so outrageous because in its radical Christian form it declares that God has chosen us even when we did not deserve it. Grace is outrageous because—in one sense—it allows nothing to us as humans.

For many of us, grace is so outrageous because it lets God be God in a way that secretly we do not want God to be God. We inwardly want—sometimes fervently desire—the wicked in the world, the scoundrels, to "get theirs!" We do not want them to "get off the divine hook." For many of us who judge ourselves to be good, we desire to make grace simply the divine approval of other good people whom we want or would like to have in our meeting or church. Although giving lip-service to radical theology of grace, we too often do not think it "fair" of God to step into the world to accept somebody who does not "deserve" it.

We want to make people work for grace, to earn this acceptance of God. This is a kind of "pull yourself up by your spiritual bootstrap" approach to spirituality. Such a perspective has more in common with a spirituality of law than of grace which Paul champions. If Paul is right, the law will lead us only to know that we are dead! A warped view of grace will simply keep the bodies in the tomb.

Truly to become a follower of Jesus is to come to know first-hand— personally—this radically outrageous grace. Having come to know it—and the freedom it delivers—will send us carrying this graceful message into the tombs of the world. With Jesus, we will issue the graceful invitation, "Lazarus, come out." "Lazarus" will have many names and will have different faces. But, always "Lazarus" will come out—come out alive, ready to live and live abundantly.

Then—as with every prodigal who returns home, returns from death to life—there will be a party. We are God's celebrants!

Live To Breathe

Someone recently asked me what I did for a living? In a flip response, I replied, "Breathe!" The answer he expected was my vocational response. Somehow my "living" is determined by what I do. If I allow this to be true, then economics dictate my identity. I am somebody only if I "earn" a living.

This would mean that retired persons become suspect. Even if they once were productive, now they are finished. Does this mean that they are not living, but only existing? And the housewife also becomes suspect. Many want her in the house—where they have determined she belongs. Then, she is judged worthless, because she is not earning a living. To determine life by economic productivity ultimately is destructive to everybody.

It is more true that I breathe for a living than that I work for a living. We could just as well ask a pig what it does for a living and it would also say, "Breathe!" Humans are not pigs, but that does not mean that we are better than pigs. We want to say pigs live, but they do not do anything for a living. Humans do both: we live and we do something for a living.

We and pigs live because we breathe. A pig has a heart and lungs and so do we. If asked about a pig's identity, we might be tempted to say that they eat for a living. How unfortunate that we humans have decided we have to work for a living! If you do not work, you are not quite human. Children, elderly, women and minorities can be declared "nobodies," if and when they do not work.

Christians should not be comfortable defining identity by work. If we do determine identity by work, then I can be "inhuman" based on economics. Christians do not want this economical determination because we know God. We know that God created us in the divine image. And then, when we blew it, God reached out in love and asked us once more to follow.

To pursue this knowing means that my primary identity is as a disciple of Jesus, the revealer of God. My worth is determined not by my job, but rather by my discipleship. It is only in this primary context of discipleship that some humans are "worth less" than others. They are not nobodies; they are "worth less" because they have not yet discovered that they are free to live. They do not have to earn a living. Life is a gift and living is not working but discipling.

Discipling is knowing that God created me and still desires me. To be a disciple is to be a friend of Jesus. To meet with this Jesus is always to encounter the God who loves me. To live in this love goes far beyond a job. To live in this love will have us seek out other humans to satisfy our need to love and to be loved. The church becomes the place where these lovers of the divine congregate.

When we look at it this way, it is difficult not to shout, "let's go to church!"

Come To 'Bethlehem'

The season of Advent and Christmas celebrates the incarnation of God as a human being in our world. Being other than us, God chose to become like us. John 1:14 is not always cited as the gospel text for this season, but it lies at the heart of what the good news is for me and for our world. "The Word became flesh and dwelt among us."

The Christmas season always comes around to give us the chance to recognize what we all know to be true, namely, the cyclical nature of our calendar. Christmas comes every year! The importance of this can be incorporated into our theology. This is a way to make the liturgical calendar come alive. What this "coming-around-again" means is that God is continuing to give us new possibilities.

In our own world where the God of Christmas continues to operate, there is a repeating quality of new births. Bethlehem is not the historical city for Jesus alone—nor the contemporary city for pilgrimages alone—but "Bethlehem" is today the fresh possibility of faith in the God who became incarnate in that Jesus.

In a world where death is always challenging life, where vitality is always being threatened by deadness, there needs to be a continual infusion of *possibility*. A possibility is what anyone who is down or tired or feeling defeated needs to be given. When one has lost, there must be a second chance or it truly is over. When we have "blown it," we need a new possibility—or any talk of redemption is nothing more than rhetoric. Finally, the Christmas story is the story of redemption.

We do not usually think of Christmas as a story of redemption, but, in its essence, Christmas is the telling about God's grace. One cannot understand the idea of a new possibility—a new chance—apart from the idea of grace. Any adult knows that in relationship there will finally need to be an opportunity for grace or the relationship will be blown. It is no different in our relationship with God.

Christmas is the narration of how God enters in a radically new way in Jesus to re-establish the possibility of relationship. In his book on spiritual direction, *Exploring Spiritual Direction,* Alan Jones talks about "the miracle that I matter." Christmas is the theological statement of that miracle that I matter.

The God who created us comes as human to redeem us. The God who existed before us and beyond us chose to become one with us in our humanity in order that we might be united with the Christ in his divinity. Christians have chosen the Biblical truth when we recognize each other as friends. The real call in Christmas is the call into relationship, the call to friendship. Giving gifts is appropriate, but giving friendship is essential. We join the spirit of the Christmas season by going into God's world once more and offering new possibilities and giving new chances.

In God's name we will say over and over, let's be friends. In this "Bethlehem" the Christmas season is any season and the place can be any place. It is always the place of *possibility.*

Winning Through Losing

"I have no belief in luck. I am not superstitious, but it is impossible when you have reached forty and are conspicuously unsuccessful, not sometimes to half-believe in a malign providence." These words from Bertram, the anti-hero in British writer Graham Greene's novel, *Loser Takes All*, elicit a nodding understanding from all of us in life who feel we have been dealt a losing hand.

Chronologically, to be forty is to be half-dead. Worse is to be forty and conspicuously unsuccessful! In the language of sports "conspicuously" unsuccessful is a blow-out! This is a failure in life everybody sees. Failure is bad enough as a private affair; as a public event it is shame-ful.

Like Bertram, we can admit our failures, but also half-believe there is a malign providence doing us in. A "half-belief" is itself a pathetic admission of uncertainty in the face of a felt resignation to an unhappy way of life. "We can't help it," the old saying goes. "Life just isn't working out." There is only a whimpering hope against a certain despair. There is no self-confidence because we do not like our "self" in which we might have some confidence. Losing seems our only confidence. In George Fox's words of despair, "when I myself was in the deep, under all shut up, I could not believe that I should ever overcome."

Bertram is suspicious and mistrustful that there is any ultimate grace to win. Warily, he knows that grace is like kindness. And in his experience, "kindness at the skin-deep level can ruin people. Kindness has got to care." Grace is the experience of caring—and it goes deeper than niceness or even self-help programs. Grace is actually learning about love—learning to love and to be loved—to win. Sometimes we only love—in the sense of hanging on to the wrong things—the loser in us.

Ironically, Bertram only wins by learning how to lose! As a gambler, he suddenly found a "system" which was winning big money but driving away his new wife—who in the novel was the real sign of hope, of winning. At this point, the grace of losing—in order to learn how to love—is realized. He offers his chips to another and quips, "but it's loser takes all...lose these for me. It's all I've got left."

Literally, this is Bertram's conversion. The malign providence has been transformed by love. Spiritually, we losers of the world must learn to gamble! All we have left is a self-image which still half-believes in this malign providence. In the transforming grace of God's love we can risk losing and experience the conversion that "loser takes all."

Then as winners, we embrace the reward of relationship as we accept Jesus' offer into friendship.

Chapter 9
Free From........Free For

The Journey Home

I had ducked my head and entered a small, already crowded thatched-roof house with dirt floors and hardly any furniture. This was a Mayan Mopan village high in the hills of southern Belize. On a bench in the middle of the larger of the two rooms lay the tiny, dead body of an Indian woman. She would be buried later that afternoon—but first, her family wanted the Jesuit priest to bless the body.

As he blessed the body according to the Roman Catholic rite, I was both very present in that moment but also letting my thoughts drift back to a moment only a few months earlier. In that earlier moment in a well-furnished North American house in the midwest lay another dead body in the middle of a rather sumptuous living room with family members gathered. This body was a man who, too, would soon be buried. Him I knew so much better than this Indian woman whom I had not actually met—except now in her death. He was my father—I had known him all my life!

Two people had died within months of each other. One female, one male—they could have represented the human race. One materially well off, the other embodied the hardships of the Third World. Both were Christians but, interestingly, by virtue of very different routes their pilgrimages had brought them to the same place: *home.*

And this is where their story becomes our story—every human's story. Life is not so much a pilgrimage to death as it is a pilgrimage through death to home. For the Christian, Lent is that time of year when we frontally face this fact—and embrace it rather than deny it. We can embrace Lent because the story of Lent begins with the fact of life—

acknowledges the fact that life inevitably leads to death, but death is merely the threshold to home.

Lent is a time of cultivating the *awareness* of life. If we never take time to develop our awareness, we will not know how to live or die or go home. In *Simply Sane* Gerald May says "much of the time, one goes about living unaware. Eyes blinded to the wonder of the immediate moment, consciousness glued to a task or lost in fantasy. As if one feels it is more comfortable to be a robot than a harassed child." No robot risks Lent!

In his powerful Lenten book, *Passion for Pilgrimage*, Alan Jones describes this season as "a time for the asking of hard questions and the facing of hard choices." Those of us who are well off, strong, healthy and successful would like to live life without Lent. If we could avoid Lent, then we could put off Good Friday! All too easily we dismiss those who are weak, poor, sick and failures—effortlessly we consign those to their pilgrimages of death. And yet, by virtue of their lives, these already know the Lenten path, they already can affirm their death—death which will bring them to their Easter: their home. Humorously, they know finally everyone will make their pilgrimage into death and, then, home.

Alan Jones quotes Charles Peguy who says, "when we reach heaven at the end of our pilgrimage, God will ask the searching question: 'Ou sont les autres?' Where are the others? The Easter promise of new life is for everyone. In this homecoming everyone is included." Lent is the opportunity for us to hear God's serious questions even before we reach home. Lent poses the pilgrimage questions: *Who really am I and where realistically am I heading?*

This is the real difference between us and the woman and man cited at the beginning of the essay. They are already home—home free. We are still on our pilgrimage—once more, standing at the headwaters of Lent—a time to ask, "who am I," and be open to the answer which the Spirit of God speaks.

As a human, I affirm I am made in the image of God. As a Christian, I recognize most fully what that image looks like in Jesus. In his book, *The Spirit of the Disciplines,* Dallas Willard characterizes the human as "a 'living being' with an animal nature, but with a vast difference—we have a nature that is suitably adapted to be the vehicle of God's likeness. *The two sides of the great human contradiction, dust and divinity, then, are set in place."*

Dust and divinity: this is the "who am I" answer appropriate to the Lenten question. Lent recognizes both the viability and frailty of my dust. My embodied spirit is viable because it is the vehicle of God's likeness. To be viable means to have a "way." As human—created in the divine image—means God has a "way" with me. My pilgrimage is my personal traveling of my own way. My way leads from dust to divinity.

To be sure, you and I will not become "God." But, we will come to be with the divinity—to be at home. And this is the answer to the second Lenten question, "where am I heading?" We are all heading home—heading for the divinity. We are being moved along the divine river of life. There we will join Indian women and white males and all other varieties of the human dust embodying God's image.

Lent is the season for questions. We now have answers. We now know from what we are free—because we know for what we are free: home!

Free To Be

"Where there's a will, there's a way." How many times I have heard this axiom, acted on it and discovered, "no way!" In fact, the apostle Paul seems to give expression to my discovery when he tells the Romans, "I can will what is right, but cannot do it." (Rom. 8:18) This is particularly difficult for one who thinks he has a strong will and who thinks that *having* a will should be sufficient to *doing* that will.

When I understand that to have a will does not always mean I can do what I will, I realize that I cannot easily say again to anyone, "where there's a will, there's a way." I realize that a "will" does not automatically mean "will power." Indeed, in his book, *Love and Will,* Rollo May helped me be careful in assuming too much about will power. May writes "'will power' expressed the arrogant efforts of Victorian man to manipulate his surroundings and to rule his own life in the same way as one would an object."

Experientially, I know that I can both have a will and know that it is impotent—powerless. And I always thought that by working harder, I could manage it! For me, this comes true when I think about making decisions. To have a will is to be able to decide—and to decide the right or the good. Such a person is perceived to be "decisive." Certainly, at one level in life this is very important. However, at another level—the level of relationship—it is not always the way to be.

I realize in relationship with another, if I always have to be "the decider," then I am in bondage—bondage to my own will and to the dependency of the other. Normally, I think we would not consider decisive persons to be in bondage, but I believe they truly can be and frequently are in bondage. Furthermore, one comes to know that in relationship, one cannot change by oneself. Remember: it is not always true that where there's a will, there's a way! I now know that if I do not have to decide, then I am *free to respond*. In fact, the escape from the bondage of always being "the decider" is not to become "indecisive," but rather to become "responsive."

In relationship, the other can have intentions to and for me. This allows me to respond and to develop a mutuality in the relationship which is healthy, freeing and maturing. A relationship is such when two are both decisive and responsive. In this sense, discipleship is the model relationship.

When Jesus offers relationship, we are given the chance to respond. Our "Yes" has implications. As we grow and are grounded in this relationship with Jesus, we can then offer relationship to each other.

There is a provocatively simple statement about freedom when Jesus is speaking to a group of Jews who have come to believe in him. He says, "if you continue in my word, you are truly my disciples, and you will know the truth, and the truth will set you free." (Jn. 8:31-2) Usually, we understand freedom in a political sense. Spiritual freedom is different...but it is always political.

Spiritual freedom always has to do with relationship. Normally, we are trained to think that freedom means independence and autonomy. In Madison Avenue images the truly free person is Clint Eastwood as the high plains drifter or the Marlboro man. Women seldom are portrayed as free. This may be because women value relationship in ways that men traditionally have not. This may suggest why friendships—relationships—teach so much about freedom.

One can illustrate how freedom is really about relationship by hearing the sentiments of Robert Capon in his book, *Hunting the Divine Fox*. Capon says that "the Word always creates. And words always create. The idiot, by definition, is simply a man who has talked himself into a world of his own." Spiritually speaking, to understand freedom simply as independence is to become an idiot. It is merely the person who has used his/her words and images to talk himself/herself into a world of their own. The idiots are the ones who have created their own world and, then, presume that is the only real world.

No—the real world is always God's world—the world created by the Word who was and is Jesus. Men and women can only know this real world by being in touch with and in relation with this creative Word. This reality opens us up to the truth of God and its freedom. As the Peace Pilgrim says, "after that, you can never go back to completely self-centered living." Self-centered living is the man or woman living idiotically in their own creation—their own world of advertisement and of fantasy.

The spiritual freedom whose features have begun to emerge is always political. It is political because it shapes me by my relationship to God and re-shapes me in my relationship to myself (my own self-image) and others. It is not political in the sense of creating me to be an American, but it is political in the re-creation of my allegiance as an active member of the heavenly city. (Heb. 11:10)

This spiritual freedom challenges my earthly allegiances by touching into a deep place in me which knows freedom is not food, drink, wealth, prestige or power. Freedom is none of these substitutes of my own idiotic attempt to create my own world and idiotically play god in that world. But, most of us like being gods in our own little kingdoms!

That is why Jesus' invitation to relationship is always an invitation to freedom. For so many of us, this is a challenge because we are not gods—so with this invitation often we feel some risk when Jesus says, "Follow me." What we can also know in our "Yes" is the joy beyond the risk—the joy which comes with that friendship with Jesus. And in that joy we are free.

'You Are Precious To Me'

The daily newspaper article begins with the words that "hundreds of prison inmates cheered, whistled and clapped..." Is this a lead-in to a rock star story? As unbelievable as it might seem, it is merely a human response to basic words to people confined for crime from Mother Teresa that "you are precious to me." She sums up her work in humble terms: "I'm just a little instrument in (God's) hands."

A saint among sinners? Yes, we outside a prison confinement would be quite quick to acknowledge she is a saint. We do not mind and, maybe even admire, an elderly woman (nun) visiting those people so long as they "pay" for what they have done. But, then, she has the audacity to suggest that "the crimes committed by the prisoners do not make them unworthy of love, adding "we are all sinners." This saintly woman certainly knows her Pauline theology. "For there is no distinction; since all have sinned and fallen short of the glory of God." (Rom. 3:22-23)

Sin is a problem for those of us who think we are good. Spare the rod and spoil the child; no pain, no gain. Sin is not always rectified by discipline; salvation is not always ours by will-power. Punishment is not always a matter of lock-ups. Crime is a societal issue; sin is a theological rupture. Punishment—we want fervently to believe—balances crime; love—dare we believe—overcomes sin.

There is a respectability to upper and middle-class American religion which is frightening. We can confuse conformity with sinlessness. We can bask in our edifices without pursuit of edification. With a rich heritage Quakers, for example, often simply clip the coupons and live off the interest. It is easy to poke fun at nuns, but soberly we can ask, where are our missionaries of charity (Teresa's order)?

Charity is only a back-door play again into that love perspective! Historically, Christians of all denominations have so known God in their lives that they, too, could say to anyone, "you are precious to me." Precious includes more than little babies and diamonds. Precious is the ability to see "that of God" in every person...and having seen it, speak to it and live into it. Diamonds are rock-star stories. For money or by theft you can have one.

Diamonds, however, is not where it's at. Religious respectability is not a spiritual guarantee. Only love is the currency of the divine-human exchange. That does not mean justice is unimportant or sin irrelevant. No, as Rosemary Haughton says in *The Passionate God,* sin is "the perversion of love...And it was the work of Jesus to make evident in his own body the ultimate unreality of evil."

We are now his body—Christ's body— in the world. With Mother Teresa, can we say to anyone, "you are precious to me?" To grow into the body of Christ means we, too, will show the world the ultimate unreality of evil. This means we work in those places where there is no love. As we learn to love, so will we learn that all can be precious to us. This is because all are precious to God.

Judging Or Judgments

"Judge not, that you be not judged." (Mt. 7:1) These words from Jesus' sermon on the mount have been generously quoted, but too often without much attention to their context or to their meaning. Frequently, what is meant is that there should be no judgment made. With this goes the implication that judging is dangerous and divisive; to "get along," Christians must not judge. There can be little more said that is more mistaken than the notion that Jesus did not make judgments and that contemporary Christians should also not make judgments.

Rather than catalogue where Jesus does judge, let us simply note in the fourth gospel the teaching of Jesus with respect to the Holy Spirit. On the evening of Easter Sunday Jesus appears to the disciples, gives them the Holy Spirit and says that "if you forgive the sins of any, they are forgiven; if you retain the sins of any, they are retained." (Jn. 20:23) This passage clearly implies there will be judging—but done from the perspective of the Spirit.

It seems the danger of the initial "judge not" passage is that it is easily employed by any of us who really prefer not being judged! If everyone in a congregation would agree to judge not, then we would all be free of judgment. Implicit here is the agreement that we all would be left to the safety of our private beliefs and actions.

What this does is offer a veneer of niceness in place of an exacting gospel of love. Alan Jones makes an appropriate observation about niceness when he says that "one of the most damaging things about the popular view of love is that it requires being nice all the time...we live in an age that would prefer the smooth lie to the hard truth. The result is that we are very poor at honoring genuine feelings and hard-won convictions." Real love is difficult and requires commitment—and commitment necessitates judgments. A

Christianity without judgment is a Christianity rendered impotent and meaningless by "good intentions."

What clearly can be seen is that a Christian movement which ceases to make judgments is one bound in a trapped state of superficiality. One can be nice and superficial, but never can one love and remain superficial. The question is not to judge or refrain from judging—but how to judge? The key is to understand the difference between judgment and judgmentalism.

In the spiritual sense, judgments are made from and on the basis of truth. Whether it is Jesus, Martin Luther, or you, judgments are made by speaking out of the truth given to us. Because of our limitations, we have to be careful about making absolute judgments...this leads to judgmentalism.

Judgmentalism is an absolute statement with no openness to either its effect or potential limitation. Judgmentalism cannot lead to love because it is not open. To make a judgment, however, is to speak from our truth with the awareness that more may be revealed and that the judgment may have an unexpected effect—on us and on others. Judgments are always clear—but open and still "connected." Judgmentalism is always clear—but always closed and "distancing."

Judgments are clarifying, revelatory and inviting. Rather than putting someone "in their place," judgments speak from our place. They invite a joining, encourage a belonging and facilitate a loving. From strangers, they seek to make acquaintances and, then, friends. In an ironical way, judgments are hospitable. They tell people where we are and invite others to show us where they are. Once, we were all strangers to the love of God through Jesus.

Just see what his judgment has wrought: a bunch of friends!

Discover God

The French philosopher, Blaise Pascal, says of human beings, "our nature consists in motion; complete rest is death." To be human, then, is to be in motion. The ultimate human question is "where am I heading?" In this sense, the human journey is always an emotional journey. *E-motion* is movement of the person by something or somebody. Life is always in motion, e-motional. This means to the ultimate question, "where am I heading," we add its twin question, "and what moves me?"

Basically, spirituality is about answering both these questions. Actually, spirituality has only one, very simple answer to both questions: God! God is the answer to where I am heading and God is the one moving me in that direction. The person who has traded selfishness for spirituality is the person who now knows that she or he is emotionally being drawn more and more into God's presence. However, so many of us are too busy living our lives our own way that we have missed God. In fact, we have declared we are our own god—we know where we are heading and we declare ourselves to be in charge!

In Catherine de Hueck Doherty's book, *Poustinia: Christian Spirituality of the East for Western Man*, she has an arresting statement for all us little gods. She says "there is but one tragedy: not to be a saint. If these motivations of life are not such that they can be true foundations for sanctity, then the soul must start all over again and find other motivations. It can be done. It must be done. It is never too late to begin again." The tragic life is the life which refuses sanctity—declines the holy invitation to the divine embrace. But, the invitation is always there; we need only be motivated to begin.

We are not born saints; we become saints. A saint is not a perfect person; a saint is one living in the Spirit, walking "in the newness of life" as Paul describes it. (Rom. 6:4) To become a saint requires what I call "incremental spirituality." We begin by taking small steps and incrementally—that is, with small increases—we give breadth and depth to our spiritual lives. There are three steps to this incremental spirituality: *discovery* (which will now be examined), *development* and *deployment* (which will be examined in the next two essays).

The first step, then, is discovery. Once more, this is fairly simple, it just is not easy! The discovery phase is that period of time and process of coming to awareness—coming to realize that we are not gods and that we accept the God who is. Discovery is the realization that life is in motion and emotionally we are heading in the right direction when we let go of control and let God move us. This is problematic because so many of us do not know how to begin. But, actually there is only one way to fail—not to begin.

One good way to begin is to find a few minutes (five or ten is initially enough) to be by yourself and be quiet (spirituality calls these *solitude* and *silence*—usually takes the place of tv's!) There is one thing now to do in solitude and silence. In the words of de Hueck Doherty you "fold the wings of (your) intellect and open the doors of (your) heart. The Russians would say: Put your head into your heart and try to achieve a deep and profound interior silence." You have done what you can and now God will do what God always wants to do—God will come, will speak, will touch and, finally, will love.

But, how do we put our head into our heart? The first understanding is to accept that our "heart" is that core part of who we are. Theophan the Recluse, a nineteenth century Russian mystic, puts it this way. "The heart is the innermost man or spirit. Here are located self-awareness, the conscience, the idea of God and of one's complete dependence on Him, and all the eternal treasures of the spiritual life...Where is the heart? Where sadness, joy, anger, and other emotions are felt, here is the heart. Stand there with attention."

To put our head in our heart, then, is to go to the real place of our "self" and attend to God who comes to visit. Our discovery will be that God is not only a visitor, but will take up residency in our lives. Discovery, then, is a way of "coming to attention"—literally, of coming to be in "tension" with the possibility that God is always desirous to move us in the direction of our divine destination. To come to attention is not to come to a rigid posture by clicking our heels and saluting, but relaxing into solitude and quietly waiting for the divine visit.

Having discovered the divine visitor, we have discovered the truth of Thomas Kelly's words from *A Testament of Devotion*. "Deep within us all there is an amazing inner sanctuary of the soul, a holy place, a Divine Center, a speaking Voice, to which we may continuously return." Thank God!

God's E-Motion

The previous issue launched a three part series on incremental spirituality—that process which enables each disciple to become a saint, a person walking in the newness of life. Spirituality is incremental because it begins with small steps and incrementally—with small increases—comes to have God's Spirit permeate more and more our lives. As that happens, we have a spirituality which answers the two human questions: "where am I heading?" and "what moves me?"

As we saw, God is the answer to both questions. Incremental spirituality is the discovery of the "amazing inner sanctuary of the soul," as Thomas Kelly described it. Discovery is the process of putting our heads in our hearts, paying attention to that divine center within. As the first step of incremental spirituality, discovery is attending to that divine within.

The second step of incremental spirituality is the intentional *development* of our discovery. This is precisely the emotional embrace of the "Christ within." E-motion, we recall, is the movement of the person by someone else—in this case, we become spiritual when God moves us—or moves in on us! John Bradshaw calls emotions "energy in motion." The second step in incremental spirituality is the development—particularly, through discipline—of our energy. The spiritual person is an *energetic* person—one who has vitality, whose step has bounce and whose eye has a glint. This is the person who knows the truth which the second century bishop, Irenaeus, proclaimed: "true life comes from partaking in God."

The key to developing this emotional energy which pulsates from God is to discipline it. Unfortunately, for many, discipline is a "negative" word which somehow always has to mean "hard" or "without fun"—too often associated with hated piano lessons or running laps for no good reason.

"You want discipline? Join the Marines!" we chuckle. But, people and books like Richard Foster's *Celebration of Discipline* and Dallas Willard's *The Spirit of the Disciplines* have helped rectify this false assumption of what discipline must be. For example, Willard shows the connection between discipline and a life with God when he states "anything with life in it can flourish only if it abandons itself to what lies beyond it, eventually to be lost as a *separate* being, though continuing to live on in relations to others. Life is inner power to reach and live 'beyond.'"

The key to releasing this inner power—this spiritual energy through development—is the elimination of the deadness in our souls. Much human energy is mis-spent buoying up lives in useless pursuits and meaningless anxieties. These are not life-producing, but death-dealing. It is like building personal nuclear bombs to inflict self-damage in the name of "protection." By eliminating this emotional nonsense, we are free to "be moved" in a more appropriate God-designated direction—to live instead of die.

Instead of armed for a fight, we are delivered into the caring arms of a re-creative God. Instead of a struggle unto death, we are liberated unto life—abundant life. Abundant life will be present where deadness begins to erode and, then, disappear. Abundant life is the fruit of spiritual discipline.

In her book, *Fullness of Life*, Margaret Miles gives contemporary Christians an idea of what spiritual discipline accomplishes in our lives. The goals of discipline "include self-understanding, overcoming of habituation and addiction, gathering and focusing of energy, ability to change our cultural conditioning, and intensification or expansion of consciousness." These words enable us to see the purpose of discipline is for the purpose of something beyond discipline—namely, for life and life abundantly.

This means we do not engage discipline to be "disciplined," but rather because discipline eliminates deadness and makes new life possible. By themselves, disciplines will not eliminate deadness, but, they put us in touch with God who does. Foster artfully notes disciplines "are a way of sowing to the Spirit. The Disciplines are God's way of getting us into the ground; they put us where He can work within us and transform us...They are God's means of grace."

Foster's words are an important reminder that, in fact, discipline is a form of grace. To be sure, there is work involved in the practice of a discipline—it requires effort and patience. But finally, if discipline is not "gracing," then it probably was not of God. We will know it is "gracing" us if we begin to see the fruit of practice. For many of us, this will take the form of Miles' observation: there will be more self-understanding, addiction will be broken, energies will be focused and available, we will grow and life will be appropriately intensified. Miles offers a contemporary language and understanding for what Jesus meant by abundant life.

You should choose you discipline based on what will be needed to grow in the presence of the discovered inner sanctuary. It may be the classical disciplines like prayer, study or fasting. Or, it might be a newer, "less obvious" discipline like self-care or group sharing.

The goal of discipline is growth—growth into the divine reality God has given us with the amazing inner sanctuary. You are alive—with discipline you can be vitally alive! Go for it!

Discovery, development and deployment: these are the three steps to incremental spirituality. In the first of this three part devotional series incremental spirituality was defined as the means by which we become saints—by taking small steps and incrementally (small increases at a time) gain breadth and depth in our spiritual lives. Incremental spirituality is always *emotional*—"e-motion," the movement of a person by God into the divine direction.

Move Into God

In his book, *The God Who Comes*, Carlo Carretto, an Italian Catholic, captures well the essence of this incremental spirituality. "It is said that the spirituality of man on earth is the spirituality of Exodus, of the long journey which stretches from the freedom up from slavery to the joys of the Promised Land, possessed and enjoyed for ever." Incremental spirituality is the *discovery* of God and the emotional, spiritual journey out of our own bondage—our personal Egypts. It is the *discipline* of the desert, the training of our journey home—home into God's arms. Finally, incremental spirituality is the *deployment* of God's Spirit throughout a world yet living in its own Egypt—bound by its own chains of slavery. Incremental spirituality culminates in our incarnational re-involvement in this "worldly Egypt"—but from the Promised Land perspective.

The Promised Land perspective is really Jesus' perspective. Indeed, to share this perspective will makes us almost like Carretto, little sisters and brothers of Jesus. This perspective knows that "God has always been coming. He came in the creation of light, and he came yet more in Adam. He came in Abraham but was to come more fully in Moses. He came in Elijah, but was to come even more fully in Jesus. The God who comes takes part in the procession of time. With history He localizes Himself in the geography of the cosmos, in the consciousness of man, and in the Person of Christ. He has come and has yet to come." Deployment, then, is living from the reality of the God who has come and giving ourselves to the world as the hope of the God who is yet to come.

This God who has been coming since the beginning of time is actually a God of deployment. The word comes from the French and means to "unfold" and "spread out."

But, there is an even more special bent to the idea of deployment. Usually, it involves a strategic unfolding. This is how one should understand God's incarnation through Jesus—a strategic, divine unfolding of grace and love. This strategic unfolding God continues in our *own* deployment in the world.

Action is the key to deployment. In another of his books, *Letters From the Desert*, Carretto describes Jesus as "the carrier of the message." Carretto elaborates. "Well, what did he do? He did not open hospitals or found orphanages. He became flesh, lived among people and he embodied the Gospel message in its entirety. *Coepit facere.* He began to act." That was his spiritual deployment. Our spiritual deployment will be our beginning to act.

We are moved. We move. We join a movement. All this is very emotional—the moving away from and the moving into. We know now where we are heading: the Promised Land. But, the Promised Land is not some geographical place over which spiritual people can fight. Rather, the Promised Land has more to do with grace than place. The Promised Land is that movement of grace—the emotional, divine deployment of God's very Self to which we have been joined. As Gerald May puts it in his book, *Addiction & Grace*, "grace is the dynamic outpouring of God's loving nature that flows into and through creation in an endless self-offering of healing, love, illumination, and reconciliation...when grace is so clearly given unrequested, uninvited, even undeserved, there can be no authentic response but gratitude and awe."

To know where we are heading is simultaneously to know that it is God who is moving me. Thomas Aquinas and countless others have described God as the "Unmoved Mover." Incremental spirituality transforms this dusty dogma into a living, breathing Person. Incremental spirituality moves us from reading to acting.

Incremental spirituality is always transformational. It is the strategic growing into the saint God wants us to be. It is the step by step, day by day wandering in wonderment. Our wandering is not aimless. It is focused; it is disciplined. It is graced. Our wonderment is not sophomoric giddiness. It is grounded in the discovery of the very depth of the universe's secret: there is a God...and that God loves *you!*

That divine love has been deployed in Jesus who delights in loving you into sainthood. That love, in turn, deploys you into a profane world. That love causes a re-action. Catch it!

Chapter 10
Suffering

Why Suffering?

In her very challenging book, *Suffering*, Dorothee Soelle begins quickly to undercut the comfortable status so many of us claim. Provocatively, she allows "the ideal of life free from suffering, the illusion of painlessness, destroys people's ability to feel anything." Particularly, through its media the First World culture extols a life free from suffering. Furthermore, it implicitly suggests that where suffering exists, you are the problem. Unfortunately, our churches are culturally co-opted by implying pain/suffering are the result of personal sin. These implications potentially carry destructive seeds for all of us.

Soelle is especially hard on those of us who think we know something theologically! "Theologians have an intolerable passion for explaining and speaking when silence would be appropriate," she laments. However, one thing is clear: how we view suffering is basically a feature of our theology (our view of God), as well as our sense of human nature. Indeed, the ideal of a life free from suffering is actually more an illusion than ideal.

The real question seems to be less *whether* there will be suffering, but more *why* is there suffering? And this pointedly implicates God as well as humans. This is exactly when theology becomes tricky and theologians need to consider the option of listening!

To engage seriously the question, *why* is there suffering, is to risk leaving the ideal world and settling into our real world where folks hurt and, in turn, often hurt others. Giving up the illusion of painlessness is to grasp reality. For the most part, this illusion is perpetuated by a male-dominated, macho-infested culture. Show us a woman who has given birth and you will see someone who has experienced pain. Perhaps, this is initially the place to see where there can be fresh movement of God's Spirit. It moves headlong into the question, why suffering?

In a rather complex manner Soelle facilitates this movement to the real place. "If the most important question addressed to suffering is whom it serves, God or the devil, becoming alive or paralysis, passion for life or the destruction of this passion, then the other question addressed to suffering, namely, that of theodicy, appears to be superseded." Theodicy—a big word—simply means God is responsible for evil and suffering.

At one level, if this is God's world, ultimately God is responsible. But, if Soelle is correct, that is not the question. The problem is not to figure out who is responsible. "Whom suffering serves" supersedes this question. Does suffering facilitate life or paralyze it? Does it energize passion for life or destroy it?

In the case of childbirth, pain and suffering clearly lead to life and even push for life. In a revealing way, we see this to be a key to the central Christian story of the passion—a story necessarily involved with suffering—a suffering unto death, so that there might be life. Soelle reminds us, "Jesus' passion is the quintessence of such freely chosen suffering." What Jesus' passion demonstrates is a way not only to allow suffering and pain to be real, but also redemptive.

Jesus' passion is the iconoclastic response to the illusion of a life free from suffering and the illusion of painlessness. The passion smashes that illusion. Jesus' passion says suffering is real: the question is whether it can be redemptive and life-giving? His was; can ours be? That may be the real question!

Cowardly, we Christians often dodge the reality of the passion for the fruit of the resurrection. This temptation assumes death is a painless transition from Madison Avenue to the golden streets of heaven. Once more, Soelle lays a roadblock to this theology when she proclaims "to be in the image of God without attaining the image of Christ is a suffering-free Christianity—which, however, means at the same time one that leaves the suffering to others." The scary part now is the challenge that to leave suffering to others is to know they have the key to Christianity and to life! It leaves me locked in my closet of illusion and the isolation of an ideal.

Actually, we have arrived at the appropriate understanding about pain and suffering when we realize—as Christians—we must take seriously being in the image of Christ and its consequent, *imitatio Christi,* the imitation of Christ. With Soelle, Christians can abandon a theological masochism and "the low value it places on human strength; its veneration of one who is neither good nor logical but only extremely powerful; its viewing of suffering exclusively from the perspective of endurance; and its consequent lack of sensitivity for the suffering of others." Here is the key: Jesus was not a masochist; he was redeemer. And the clarity of his call to discipleship is the invitation to involvement.

His call to involvement is a call to be real: to know there is suffering and pain. Christianity is the iconoclastic word to the stupidity of secular culture. Our Christian call is not to avoid the reality of suffering and pain, but it is a call to the sensitivity for the suffering of others. Our call is not to flee but to be free—free to others in their pain. The real God alleviates pain where possible and transforms suffering when there is not another way. Our call is no less.

Heal, don't hurt.

Spiritual Vulnerability

"To be" is to be vulnerable. To be vulnerable means to be subject to injury or hurt. Vulnerability is the disposition for woundedness. Human beings would like to live life pretending that they are not vulnerable—hoping that there will be no hurt, avoiding the possibility of being wounded. The lure of life, however, is always the call to vulnerability.

It is only as one learns that vulnerability is ultimately the way to God (and, consequently, to meaning in life), that one can choose to embrace vulnerability. One can be vulnerable at four levels: physically, emotionally, intellectually, and spiritually. It is easiest to describe the physical vulnerability. Physical vulnerability knows that health is its opposite, sickness its sign and death its fear. Emotional vulnerability is the threat that my feelings may be hurt. We fear being "wiped out." Intellectual vulnerability means appearing "stupid" or "wrong." Ultimately, it means my perspectives and thoughts are senseless—nobody wants to be with somebody so dumb!

Spiritual vulnerability allows us to feel—and to know that our meaning comes from beyond ourselves. To be spiritually vulnerable means we risk death, risk being wiped out, risk stupidity—all to discover life itself. Vulnerability is the process of risking the old self to be given the new self. To be vulnerable is to know what Paul meant when he said, "if any one is in Christ, he is a new creation; the old has passed away, behold, the new has come." (II Cor. 5:17)

This kind of spiritual vulnerability to God and to God's reconciling work through Christ leads in two ways to the emerging of ourselves as new creatures. In the first place, our vulnerability to God calls us to risk the societal images we have created—or accepted—for ourselves. Some of us see ourselves as smart and strong—others of us see ourselves as unable and weak. Some think we are great and others see us as born losers. Spiritual vulnerability risks all these self-imposed and self-accepted images.

In the second place, as we risk these images, we will discover our real self-image emerges. The real self is the selfcreated in the image of God and now, through the vulnerability to God's reconciling work, restored to that image of God. The image of God replaces the societal image. We are now given the space and the grace to emerge as the new creature living in the world, to be sure, but rooted in the Spirit.

To be rooted in the Spirit is the key. If this happens, vulnerability is no longer a threat. The world can hassle us—society can buffet us—but we shall overcome. We are grounded in a divine reality which protects us from ultimate harm and which provides nurture and nourishment which erodes hassle with serenity and buffeting with peace.

May our prayer be that we make ourselves vulnerable to this kind of God.

Creation And Chaos

"The present generation of Christians must learn to live with chaos: it is a providential vocation." These telling words from the book of the Anglican theologian, Martin Thornton, *Prayer: A New Encounter*, speaks powerfully to those of us who want to be open to our own lives—aware of real life. In our own time, we have looked chaos in the eye. Scud missiles zooming towards Israel made every person shudder. Would the Israelis, in turn, retaliate to begin the "big one?" The break up of the USSR provided another glimpse of chaos. Closer to home, each of us can look inwardly and always see the potential chaos in our own lives. The question in the face of our faces is: do we want to learn to live with it?

Far too many of us simply do not. Thornton continues by saying, "I have deep sympathy with the conservatives who have been faithful to the old ways and who view the present upheaval with apprehension and distrust. Why change anyway? Why cannot the wretched theologians leave things alone?" Actually, the problem is not with the "wretched theologians," but with the persons about whom theologians talk: God and God's children—us! The problem is being human! To be human means we are created—means we are not naturally gods. To be human means we are naturally and inevitably threatened with chaos.

Chaos is always a threat to creation. When we understand the link between creation and chaos, then we gain a profound sense for the role chaos plays in our lives. Genesis is our appropriate beginning point. Fascinatingly, Genesis begins with the statement about creation rather than chaos. "In the beginning God created the heavens and the earth." (Gen. 1:1) This suggests the very nature of God is "creative." God brings the world and humans into being ("genesis" itself means "beginning"). Only against this genesis—this creation—does chaos come to have value.

After the statement of creation Genesis continues: "the earth was without form and void, and darkness was upon the face of the deep; and the Spirit of God was moving over the face of the waters." (Gen. 1:2) So, to have a sense for what chaos is gives a more definitive sense for creation. We better understand creation over against chaos—and chaos is always a possibility for creation gone awry.

The English word, "chaos," is a transliteration of the Greek, *chaos*. Chaos is rude, unformed mass; it is infinite space, empty space, a gulf. Our English word, "chasm," serves appropriately to describe chaos. As the Genesis text says, chaos is to be without form and to be void, to be empty. Chaos threatens creation by dragging creation back into a formless and empty place. To be in chaos is not to go out of existence—to become nothing. To be in chaos is worse because one is in *chaos*, which means *to be*, but to be *empty*. To be in chaos is to be in confusion, in darkness, in despair.

To understand chaos in this way enables us better to grasp what Thornton means when he says we have to learn to live with chaos. Insofar as we humans are created (and we are!), we will have to face chaos. Not to learn to live spiritually with it means chaos will erode us into emptiness and meaninglessness. We will come to be less than human—less than what God creatively intended.

Most of us will not experience cosmic chaos, but almost all of us experience our own inner chaos. Problems with illness, teen-agers, spouses, parents, teachers, friends, bosses—all these are constant sources of potential chaos. Probably, even more, our own "selves" can also be sources of inner chaos. Often, we are so adept at self-inducing chaos, we need no outside help! Simultaneously, we do in our own creativity and our creative potentiality as God's creatures.

A noted physician and author, Willard Gaylin, puts it this way in his *Adam and Eve and Pinocchio*. "Almost all psychic distress is the product of a distorted perception that transforms our present reality, undervalues our strengths, and anticipates a dreaded imagined doom that tragically may arrive—precisely and only because it is anticipated." Few of us worry about the atomic bomb; all of us can bomb our inner selves into the chaos of individual and corporate doomsday. We launch our own scuds into the hearts of our lives!

To learn to live with chaos is a providential vocation. As human, every one of us has this vocation—this "calling." The calling is creatively to live with chaos and spiritually to turn it into abundant life. Every day our call is to walk into the life which God has generatively given us and to make meaning with our lives. We will be providentially guided in this process by God's hand. Providence is the ongoing creative hand of God on us—we who are God's creatures.

Historically, many Christians have talked about God in providential terms. God works "'with" us rather than "forcing" us. Providence is God's will calling us (vocation) in order that the created world share in the divine reality, the divine creativity, the divine order, and the divine beauty." Our response to God's providential call is a daily "Yes." It is our response to be creative rather than destructive, to bring order to the potential chaos and to live beautifully in a world which too easily becomes ugly.

Believe it: we are beautiful spiritual roses!

Jesus The Messiah

Christians have a treasure in our Jewish foundation and heritage. One of our Christian tragedies is the way we misuse—or even abuse—that Jewish heritage. For example, to Christians it is the "Old Testament"; to the Jew it is the "Bible." Christians can learn to call it the "Hebrew Bible." This is more than a difference in language—a semantic variation. This represents the significant overlap of our two traditions and indicates an essential difference on a theological level. As a Christian, I have been led to dialogue with my Jewish brother and sister about "their" Bible which I find to be a "part" of my own Bible. Rather than putting them in their place, I want to try to find what their place is.

Essential to the differences between the Jew and the Christian is the person of the Messiah. One could be simplistic and tongue-in-cheek say the difference merely is one of grammatical tenses. The Jew still speaks about the Messiah with the future tense, "will be." The Christian has changed the future tense to present tense, "is." Furthermore, the present Christian awareness of the Messiah carries with it the knowing that the Messiah is Jesus. It is precisely the difference in how we deal with the Messiah that makes such a rich possibility for dialogue. If Jew and Christian had no common conception of Messiah, the possibility for rich interchange would not even be present.

I have learned from the dialogue. A Jewish Hasidic master shares the following: "Basing myself on the Talmudic saying that if all men repented, the Messiah would come, I decided to do something about it. I was convinced I would be successful. But where was I to start? The world is so vast. I shall start with the country I know best, my own. But my country is so very large. I had better start with my town. But my town, too, is large. I had best start with my street.

No: my home. No: my family. Never mind, I shall start with myself." If Rabbi Shmelke begins with himself to repent, this sets in motion a movement to bring the Messiah.

I can logically imagine that. What I have experienced as a Christian, however, is the exact opposite. Rather than "following up" with the Messiah, God, as Jesus, chose in the midst and flow of history to "step in" and transform history. In this sense, Jesus is not the "messianic sequel" as much as the messianic *initiator*.

But, history really is transformed only insofar as I am transformed. It makes a difference to affirm "Jesus is Lord," only if there is a resulting transformation. Then, I know that I have been changed. Then, like Rabbi Schmelke, I can begin with the street, town, country and world. Instead of starting a process which will lead up to the coming of the Messiah, I have responded and have joined the friends of Jesus to live out the Messiah's presence.

As Jesus' friends, we are agents of the Messiah. We will help lead the world to know the Messiah—know that the Messiah not only "will be" but the Messiah "already is." As friends of Jesus, we go into the world to feed the hungry, to give clothes to the naked and justice to the oppressed. When we do this, the world will truly know the Messiah already has come.

Why are we waiting?

Fresh Winds Are Blowing

There are fresh winds of God's Spirit! Wherever God is, there will always blow fresh winds. For so many of us, the tragic state is we miss this blessing. Then, we wonder, where is God? Or, some of us have fixed up ourselves so nicely, we complain about the wind messing up our spiritual hair! Others are afraid of the gusty blowings of God's Spirit, so we take refuge in our houses of isolation or churches of security. That way, we can watch the strong winds comfortably through a window.

There are fresh winds of the Spirit! And it is only in the wind that there is life. Both Hebrew and Greek translate the same word as wind and spirit. So, to be in the wind is to be in the Spirit. The creation of humankind originated with this divine "in-breathing,"—this original, creative gust of Spirit—which animated and energized the dust from the ground. Genesis narrates that "the Lord God formed man of dust from the ground, and breathed into his nostrils the breath of life; and man became a living being." (Gen. 2:7)

There are fresh winds of the Spirit! This creative act is the highest form of divine inspiration. Literally, "inspiration" means *in-spiritus*, in the spirit or wind. Creatively, God put the spirit into the lifeless form of a human and that form became a living being. Creation is an inspirational miracle. Human beings are living miracles! And yet, we seldom know it, appreciate it or celebrate it. To do so, would make us spiritual. Spirituality is nothing more than coming to see with our miraculous eyes and celebrating the God who has given us life.

There are fresh winds of the Spirit! But we forget. In his book, *The Living Reminder*, Henri Nouwen tells a story from Elie Wiesel, a Jewish holocaust survivor. In 1944, he, along with others from a Hungarian town, Sighet, was sent to a concentration camp. Twenty years later Wiesel returned to

Sighet to find no trace of Judaism. Wiesel reflected, "I was not angry with the people of Sighet...for having driven out their neighbors of yesterday, nor for having denied them. If I was angry at all it was for having forgotten them. So quickly, so completely...Jews have been driven not only out of town but out of time as well." This trenchant story about the Jews is, sadly, also the story of God. Not only has God been driven out of our world but out of time as well. God is not remembered.

But, there are fresh winds of the Spirit! There is a fresh blowing of God's Spirit and we, like the exiled Israelites of Ezekiel's vision, are in the midst of a valley full of dry bones. Too many of us have gone AWOL from God's presence; we have become exiles from Jesus' kingdom and we remain foreigners to faith. But, we also are in the place where we can hear for ourselves the words God addressed to Ezekiel in the prophetic vision: "Can these bones live?" (Ez. 37:3) Speaking further, God surely is in the context of re-creation: "Prophesy to these bones, and say to them, O dry bones, hear the word of the Lord...Behold, I will cause breath (wind) to enter you, and you shall live." (Ez. 37:5)

There are fresh winds of the Spirit! Those winds are blowing new life into old, dry, frustrated, depressed, egocentric bones. To those who are sad, the wind blows with joy. To those who are bitter, the wind blows sweetly. The wind can always be felt where we are, as we are and pick up our soul. In the fifth century the monk, John Cassian, records in his *Conferences* the words of Abba Isaac who compares our soul to a feather. "There is a good comparison between the soul and a delicate little feather. If a feather has not been touched by damp, it is so light that the slightest breath of wind can puff it high into the air. But if even a little damp has weighted it down, it cannot float, and falls straight to the ground." Too many souls are dampened by life, too weighed down to live, too heavy freely to float. For heavy souls like this, there needs to be another miracle, a pentecostal miracle.

There are fresh winds of the Spirit! But too many are too ready to hide behind doors of fear—like the disciples on resurrection Sunday evening. We often cower in life's darker corners. But, that is exactly where the miracle of Pentecost happens when that re-creating Spirit once again freshly blows. John's gospel records the miracle this way: "Jesus came and stood among them and said to them, 'Peace be with you'...And when he had said this, he breathed on them, and said to them, 'Receive the Holy Spirit.'" (Jn. 20:19,22)

There are fresh winds of the Spirit! Like God, we are invited to come and ride the wings of the wind. Spirituality is learning to ride—it is learning to float effortlessly like the feather. Take a deep breath—that is your breath, that is God's gift. Receive the Spirit—that is your life, that is God's gift. There are fresh winds of the Spirit and your world has a whole new smell.

Come out of your house—come out of yourself. Live!

Treasure For Trash

In his book, *Leaving Home,* Garrison Keillor observes that "life is complicated and not for the timid. It's an experience that when it's done, it will take us a while to get over it. We'll look back on all the good things we surrendered in favor of deadly trash and wish we had returned and reclaimed them." Cynically, one could read this passage as an argument for purgatory!

Purgatory would function as a kind of half-way house between death and heaven—a space where we are spending some time getting over our lives. In this sense, purgatory is not a theological doctrine, but a spiritual experience of transition—transition from life to eternal life.

This spiritual experience will be a place of some sadness and grief. As Keillor says, we will look back on all the good things we surrendered in favor of deadly trash. There can be no deadly trash in heaven—space with God. Again, heaven is less a theological doctrine and more a descriptive word for the human and cosmic presence with God. So, purgatory is not a Roman Catholic doctrine, so much as a grief process for those life experiences where we opted for deadly trash.

Our point in hearing Keillor is not to create a non-Roman Catholic doctrine of purgatory, but to recognize that what Keillor says is so true about life. Life is where we are under temptation to surrender the good things for trash. Particularly, Americans and citizens of the First World are fantastic generators of trash. Our lives are complicated and our trash is symbolic of life wastefully lived. Ours has become the microwave society—rooted in a throw-away mentality where the trash bag is the mortal symbol of the culmination of the consumptive process. "Out of sight, out of mind" became the twentieth-century slogan. That does not prevent trash; it simply and tragically ignores it!

Once more, the words on life by Keillor have a bite. Cynically, he notes "every time I read a book about how to be smarter, how not to be sad, how to raise children and be happy and grow old gracefully, I think, 'Well, I won't make those mistakes, I won't have to go through that,' but we all have to go through that. Life isn't a vicarious experience. You get it figured out and then one day life happens to you. You prepare yourself for grief and loss, arrange your ballast and then the wave swamps the boat." We cannot prepare ourselves for grief and loss because when the waves swamp the boat, then we will have to *experience* grief and loss.

Death, defeat, disease, depression, despair—these boat-swampers come causing loss and producing grief. Their coming is not questioned; the question is whether there can be hope—whether on this side of purgatory we can learn something about a life which can never *finally* be swamped?

In Christian terms, the question is always an Easter question: the Christian answer affirms *one can know life* before death—in spite of defeat, in contrast to disease, above depression and in place of despair. This is life lived in touch with that deeply divine place in every one of us where even—before the death experience—it is all put together. As Annie Dillard says in *Teaching a Stone to Talk*, this is "the unified field: our complex and inexplicable caring for each other and for our life together here. This is given. It is not learned." This unified field is where all of us—those who have been cleansed and taught by purgatory experience—gather to live and to love.

This unified field is where God's presence is always present. And we know it because people have quit trashing themselves and each other. It is where we choose the good instead of surrendering it. But, we have to be careful how we define "good" things. That is the mistake so many in the First World make: we simply define whatever we do, think, believe or desire as good. Then by definition, we are good! If we are so good, why is there so much trash! We are insulated by our definition and isolated by our desecration. We are on guard because deep in us is this caring for each other. It's a given. Sadly, we have better learned how to be trashers.

God's presence continues actively transforming the trash. It is evident whenever and wherever someone "takes care." This presence is evident when someone takes care of herself. It is just as evident when someone takes care for another. We are brought into heaven when we discover the good life and enjoy it. This is the hope.

To feel this hope is to be renewed and revitalized. In the words of Keillor, it is to be awakened to "thank you, God, for this good life and forgive us if we do not love it enough." To love life is to come close to heaven—where finally God "will wipe away every tear from their eyes, and death shall be no more, neither shall there be mourning nor crying nor pain any more." (Rev. 21:4)

So, love life! Do not regret it. Celebrate it!

Can We Be Present?

In his book, *On Beginning From Within,* Douglas Steere's final words come in a quotation from Unamuno: "Sow yourselves, sow the living part of yourselves, in the furrows of life." Somehow these words remind me of the similar words of Jesus to the multitude that "whoever would save his life will lose it; and whoever loses his life for my sake and the gospel will save it." (Mk. 8:35) This is an appropriate Christmas text.

What we have to give at the Christmas season is not our presents or good cheer—but literally ourselves. The world does not need another necktie or perfume, but the world could use our love poured out in service of our lives. The season of Christmas celebrates the gift of God as person—as baby Jesus, as compassionate Lord, as resurrected life-giver. Jesus was God's gift of the divine self poured out in loving service.

When I think about how I may give myself to the world, two possibilities emerge. Both are legitimate. The first way of giving myself is what seems to be the clearest example of *imitatio Christi*—the imitation of Christ. The first way is giving is to be *vulnerable.*

It strikes me that the chief characteristic of the God–person, Jesus Christ, is that he is vulnerably available to the world. He was so available to men and women that he threatened and frightened as many as he rescued and saved! It was the frightened group which rejected him and, eventually, killed him. To be vulnerable means to be capable ourselves of being wounded. Jesus was vulnerable.

Even the birth story narrates his vulnerability. "An angel of the Lord appeared to Joseph in a dream and said, 'Rise, take the child and his mother, and flee to Egypt, and remain there till I tell you; for Herod is about to search for the child to destroy him." (Mt. 2:13) It is interesting that those surrounding him also share that vulnerability. To imitate Jesus is to be vulnerable to the "Herods" of our world. In this instance, it is important that Joseph went to Egypt and protected Jesus from the harm of premature vulnerability. This says there are right times and right places for us to be vulnerable. God asks for discipleship, not spiritual suicide!

I think Joseph spared Jesus from a "premature Herod" in obedience to the angel of the Lord—because Jesus needed for a time to be present in the world. This is the second way of giving myself to the world. The presence of Jesus was both challenging and nurturing. From this, one can conclude that our life of following Jesus is a life lived as a "present of God"—"presence of God" in the world. I am present to people by listening to them, by attending to them and sharing with them. I am God's gift in the world by being present to God's people.

There are times when my presence means vulnerability—but it does not mean that I need always to be living so that I get hurt. There will be times when we need Joseph or Mary to take us away—or remind us now is not the time for vulnerability. Our Josephs and Marys today likely will be our friends, those upon whom we depend for openness and honesty—those to whom we always are vulnerable!

To know the difference between vulnerability and being present and when to exercise each is to learn how we can lose our lives for Jesus' sake. To lose it for this is to save it. This means that we have been saved. Salvation language does not sit well with many people today. But, if we listen to the words of Dorothy Devers in *Faithful Friendship* a person can know what it means to find salvation. "By salvation I mean first of all the full discovery of who himself really is. Then I mean something of the fulfillment of his own God-given powers, in the love of others and of God."

Jesus The Inviter

Christmas is the discovery and fulfillment of persons. Ironically, by vulnerability and presence—by giving—we actually become inheritors. The giver discovers the fulfillment of the Gift.

As I have recently been in other people's offices, restaurants and other places, I have come to be aware of intrusions. An intrusion is something or someone which comes between—which invades the space between me and the other person. The term, "invades," captures well the power of the word intrusion. Intrusion is the forcing or pushing in or upon something or someone. For example, I continue to be amazed at how a "personal" conversation I am having with someone can be interrupted by the ringing telephone. I am left almost in mid-phrase while the other answers the phone.

I have often done this to friends or others in my own study! I am amazed at how we all are conditioned to respond to a ringing mechanism. We will leave someone of importance to answer a telephone often with someone on the other end who wants us for no good reason. Or, a clerk in a store giving me "personal" attention will turn around and conduct business over the phone. This makes me wish I had called!

The telephone is convenient to illustrate the nature of intrusions—only because it is simple and, therefore, easy to understand how the phone is intrusive. The phone is an easy illustration, but yet it also illustrates the difficulty of intrusions. Once an intrusion has forced or pushed its way between us, it cannot be just ignored or dismissed as if it were not there. A ringing telephone keeps ringing until answered. Oh, of course, there are ways technologically to "fix it," but an intrusion is something that has already forced its way between us. When I have been intruded upon. I want to say, "but wait a minute; am I not important right now?" How, then, do I deal with an intrusion?

I want someone with his or her phone ringing simply to say, "You are more important right now. Ignore the phone." Even if I can not concentrate on what we were saying until it stops ringing, I have received a powerful message: I have been cared for and I matter. Right now, I am more important than "the intruder." On the other hand, I begin to realize that I need to look for ways to be present and stay present for those in my presence. If my phone rings, why is the "unknown caller" more worthy of my attention than the person with whom I find myself right now?

As I ponder more about the nature of intrusion, I realize nothing—or no one—can be intrusive if I have invited or given permission for them to come into my space. This leads me to imagine Jesus was not an intruder, but an inviter. He seemed to deal with people straight and was attentive and personal. He was assertive, but not intrusive. This is an important difference. Jesus could be assertive, because he knew where he was heading—the kingdom. In fact, his ministry was his assertion: "The time is fulfilled, and the Kingdom of God is at hand..." (Mk. 1:15).

Although today Jesus would probably use a telephone, when he meant business, he would always personally call on us. It would be a personal call because Jesus invites us to do something with our lives. Intrusions put us off—they block us and irritate us. Invitations are openings—they offer embrace and belonging.

So, when you receive a call, answer expectantly. It may well be an invitation to join the kingdom-club!

"Eye-On-The-Ball"

A line from my favorite non-spiritual magazine, *Sports Illustrated*, states the obvious. The former Chicago White Sox manager, Jeff Torborg, was commenting on a coach's "eye-on-the-ball approach to hitting." He said, "when you see the ball, you have a better idea where it is." That is so obvious one would not even think about saying it! But, maybe that is the secret. One combines the natural talent and, then, attends to the "obvious." Perhaps, it is the obvious which is so often overlooked, slighted or slightly altered.

To mix baseball and spirituality can be illustrative because most Christians assume we know something about the "eye-on-the-ball" approach to spiritual living. But, whenever the too-learned spirituals among us become too sure we know the spiritually obvious, it is time to recall Dorothee Soelle's earlier-quoted words from her book, *Suffering*. She quips, "theologians have an intolerable passion for explaining and speaking when silence would be appropriate."

Soelle goes on to state things which—given the way so many of us live our spiritual lives—are not so obvious. Soelle says, "contemporary Christianity is the suffering-free religion for a world perceived as without suffering. It is the religion of the rich, the white, the industrious nations. Its God is a mild and apathetic being. In this religion suffering is shrunken down into a purely personal affair without general interest."

Suffering may be spiritually an odd place to begin talking about the "obvious." Normally, suffering does not concern us—except when a close friend enters the final stages of cancer or when a loved one meets an unfortunate accident. But, it may be this is exactly what Soelle is getting at by stating the obvious—which so many of us, as Christians, have overlooked, slighted or slightly altered. In a most challenging way, she charges that "exploitation needs a certain amount of apathy in order to run its course smoothly."

What Soelle does for those of us who are normal Christians at ease in our world is to name the obvious. God may have so loved the world that Jesus was given—and taken—and risen. But, I am not so sure I love the world in any passionate, divine way like that! The "eye-on-the-ball" approach to spiritual living is the message of the life and teaching of Jesus. These teachings and approaches are not secret; indeed, they are obvious. In fact, it is because they are so obvious that we too often must overlook, slight or slightly alter them to fit our condition. To become a friend of this Jesus begins to give many of us mixed feelings. We want to become friends—that is obvious; but obviously to do so could mess us and our world up. And so, instead of being transformed by Jesus, we transform Jesus!

Having transformed Jesus, we can now relax and settle down in a comfortable world of our own making. No longer is Jesus the God-incarnate. We have resumed our role of being "minor gods." We have reduced him to our image and domesticated him—he now lives in our house! But, through all of this now "domestic," spiritual living, there is a still, small voice of the real Jesus calling us—the real part of us that still desires to respond to his authentic call.

This call is always like the Advent season leading up to Christmas. It is the season of expectation—leading inevitably to fulfillment. In *The Genesee Diary* Henri Nouwen says "it is indeed primarily a season of joy. It is not, like Lent, primarily a time of penance. No, there is too much anticipation for that. All-overriding is the experience of joy." To be in Advent is like seeing the ball; we always are better hitters when we see the ball.

Jesus gives us these "eyes." With him we are always ready—anticipation—for the season of joy. Look: here he comes!

Conclusion

Through many devotional moments I am again and again reminded that the basic call of Jesus is to be a friend. Often we are put off by the majestic titles of Lord, Christ, Son of God and others which are attributed—rightly so—to the one in whom God was incarnate. But for me, the invitation to friendship with Jesus is the most inviting path into the spiritual life—a call to follow him. To follow him is to learn about life and love as he knew it from the creative and redemptive God, his parent. The call to follow Jesus is the call into the unity of love and life which God bestowed on the Son, Jesus.

In his farewell prayer before the crucifixion Jesus petitioned God to include us all in this circle of spiritual unity, this band of friends. In a deeply touching manner Jesus prays, "I in them and thou in me, that they may become perfectly one..." (Jn. 17:23) When Jesus invites us to be friends, it is not so much an invitation to Christian life as it is to abundant life.

And yet, so many of us experience life much as the chuckle comic in the local newspaper would have it. "Do you ever feel like life is a long elegant banquet, and you're fast food taken out in a paper sack?" When we live our lives as "fast food"—prepared routinely and homogeneously sacked for lonely consumption—we have not stepped into the circle of spiritual friendship which Jesus offers.

Jesus prays further to God. "I desire that they also, whom thou hast given to me, may be with me where I am.." (Jn. 17:24) While this finally may be a prayer for eternal life—in John's gospel, at least—eternal life begins now, begins when one "knows" the "only true God and Jesus Christ" whom God sent. Amazingly, eternal life begins in friendship. Friendship is a response to an invitation, an answer to a call. Friendship is born of desire and lived in love.

Friendship—in this vocational sense (*vocatio* = a call, an invitation)—is a journey of grace. As we cited earlier these words from *Addiction and Grace*, we do well to remember Gerald May's sentiments: "grace is the active expression of God's love. God's love is the root of grace; grace itself is the dynamic flowering of this love; and the good things that result in life are the fruit of this divine process." Adding to this Thomas Merton's notation that "our real journey in life is interior; it is a matter of growth, deepening, and of an ever greater surrender to the creative action of love and grace in our hearts." Jesus' invitation to friendship is always an invitation to journey deeper into our hearts so that we may with him go out further in compassion. Friendship is the continual transformation of desire into delight, the transfusion of renewal into the routine.

Merton says, "as for me, the job of renewal boils down to the conversion of my own life." The conversion of life is the way of grace which teaches those of us living our lives as "fast food" in sacks how to learn to live life as a long, elegant banquet. Jesus takes all of his friends into this nurturing communion. It is appropriate to end on a eucharistic note—a sacramental note.

The real key, however, is to realize we do not "take" communion so much as we "live in" communion. Quakers have realized this for centuries and have this to teach other Christians. We live in communion when we live under the canopy of light and love. There we are in the right place and space to know God, to be fed by God and to be led by God. It is a canopy experience. It is the gathering place of all the friends of Jesus. There is always room. It is the place of Maranatha—a place where our Lord has come!